TAILWINDS

HOW LOVE, FAITH AND A FUTURE SAINT LIFTED AN AIRMAN THROUGH WWII

By Martin J. Haumesser

NFB Publishing
Buffalo, New York

Copyright © 2020 Martin J. Haumesser

Printed in the United States of America

TAILWINDS: HOW LOVE, FAITH AND A FUTURE SAINT

LIFTED AN AIRMAN THROUGH WWII/ Haumesser— 1st Edition

ISBN: 978-1-7338764-5-2
     1. Title.
     2. World War II.
     3. Buffalo, New York.
     4. Biography.
     5. Padre Pio
     6. US Air Force (WWII)
     7. Haumesser.

NFB
NFB Publishing/Amelia Press
119 Dorchester Road
Buffalo, New York 14213

For more information visit Nfbpublishing.com

DEDICATION

To my father, for his service to his country, his love for his family, and his faith in God inspired by his extraordinary experiences with Padre Pio –St. Pio of Pietrelcina.

For my children, nieces and nephews, so that they may know their grandfather's story and share it with their own children some day. Pray, hope and don't worry.

Table of Contents

AUTHOR'S NOTE

If someone told you that they had met an Italian priest who bore the wounds of Jesus Christ in his hands and feet and was known to perform miracles, you might, understandably, be skeptical.

But if that someone happened to be your father, you would probably be more likely to believe him. That was my experience in writing this story.

While serving in World War II, my father had several encounters with Padre Pio, now St. Pio of Pietrelcina in the Catholic Church. I wrote this book to tell my dad's story – about his war experiences and the love he shared with my mother back home, then his fiancé. In the process, I realized how influential Padre Pio was on my father and I have attempted to make the saint central to the story.

My intention is not to sensationalize St. Pio or make believers out of skeptics. Rather, as the book's title suggests, there were tailwinds that carried my father through the war – and life – and meeting Padre Pio may have been the strongest of them all.

No matter what you believe, I think there is much to learn from this unique story. If it inspires hope, all the better. May you enjoy reading the book as much as I did writing it.

Prologue

CHAPLAIN GEORGE RICE hated this part of the job.

"Haumesser! Where's Haumesser?" the Army captain shouted as he walked among the tents scattered across the cold, muddy air base. Oil heaters warming the tents belched black smoke, casting even darker shadows on an already gray morning.

When Arthur Haumesser emerged from the warmth of his tent, he immediately felt the chill. "I'm Haumesser, sir," the airman called out.

"Come take a ride with me, son," the chaplain said somberly.

A cold November wind was blowing as Rice, a Catholic priest, stopped the jeep at the side of a lonely dirt road in the Italian countryside. He looked at the young soldier for a moment while he searched for the right words. He decided to tell it straight.

"Arthur, your father was hit by a car back home in Buffalo," the priest explained gently. "He's dead – but I'm sorry, sergeant, you can't go home. You are needed here."

The chaplain had taken the young soldier away from the base to provide some privacy in breaking the news. Arthur "Art" sat numb for an agonizingly long time, trying to process what he had just heard, the cold adding to the sting of raw emotion. He had arrived in Italy just a few weeks before, in October of 1944. And he had already witnessed the terror of war on a couple of bombing missions.

Art was an airman with the United States 15th Air Force, serving as a radio operator and gunner on a B-17 bomber in World War II. His crew flew in raids out of southern Italy to bomb Nazi targets in Germany.

There was no time to grieve for his dad. There was evil to be defeated.

Arthur was my father. This is his story.

CHAPTER 1 – LOVE LETTERS

"OH, BUT THIS has been a wonderful day! Yes, you guessed it! I received your first letter from overseas today!" – Ruth

"Oh boy, oh boy, oh boy, oh boy!!!!!! What a wonderful day I had today! Why this sudden outburst? Well, today I received 15 letters, eleven (11), I repeat, eleven from the one person I want to hear from most!" – Art

In today's text-in-a-second world, it's hard to imagine such excitement over receiving some letters. But that's how much word from home meant to the soldiers fighting across the seas against Germany and Japan in World War II. It was equally exciting – and reassuring – for loved ones on the home front to receive a letter from the soldiers so far away.

My father and mother had written those words to each other when he was in the thick of the fighting that would ultimately lead to Nazi Germany's defeat.

My family enjoys the great fortune of having all the letters that our mom and dad exchanged during the war. They were engaged after Art was drafted and the two corresponded religiously, generating a trove of correspondence that reads like a love story, a history lesson, and a unique tale of faith.

In his prescient wisdom, my father had kept all the letters in neat, chronological order in an old cardboard box. Now yellowed and worn, the letters are sweet, sometimes corny, but most often real-time accounts of life in the wartime 1940s. They give great insight into a very different era when two young lovers kept their love alive through the written word. Not only do the letters provide a glimpse into my young parents, they capture war history in the very words of those who lived it.

As you read through these chapters, text taken directly from the letters is in quotations and marked either Art for my father or Ruth for my mother. Her letters from the states help paint a picture of life on the home front.

"Say, I didn't tell you about the big celebration Buffalo is having for the Sixth War Loan* did I? Well, they have flags of all the allied countries flying from the store fronts on Main Street. They start at Seneca, I think, and go up as far as the shows. It's really a pretty sight. Then, at Lafayette Square, they have a huge replica of the Liberty Bell and anyone who buys a bond is privileged to ring the bell." – Ruth

His letters from overseas give the soldier's perspective.

"So now we have a new president, or, rather in my case, a new commander-in-chief. I heard it first in the chow line this morning and didn't quite believe it, but it's true. Roosevelt was a good man and a fine president. It will take a very capable man to fill his place." – Art

The letters my father sent home are each stamped "Passed by Army Examiner" with the signature of Lieutenant Campbell. Security concerns meant that soldiers could not give away their whereabouts or where they might be headed in combat. Every letter was scanned for possible censorship.

"Loose lips sink ships" was a phrase on war posters to remind soldiers and American citizens that careless talk – in letters, on the telephone, etc. – could jeopardize the war effort. But that didn't stop my father from giving great details in his letters of what fighting a war was like so far from home.

There were more than 500 letters sent between my dad and mom from early 1943 to the fall of 1945! And those 500 are pretty evenly split between the two of them. I won't write 250 letters to anyone in my lifetime, and they

managed to do it over a couple of years.

An upside down stamp on the envelope was their little secret message of "I love you". My mother said her younger brother, Roy, who was not quite ten, would always point out the upside down stamp as a mistake, not understanding it was done on purpose.

I have read every letter. Like so many World War II veterans, my father didn't speak a lot about the harrowing experiences he encountered. But in his letters, I found a compelling story as he faithfully wrote home and described his many distinct experiences in Italy.

Among the wickedness of war, Art also wrote about the goodness he found in a mystic priest named Padre Pio living in a mountain monastery in Italy. Growing up, we heard about Padre Pio from our father, but in reading the letters, I learned for the first time how he had interacted with the priest on numerous occasions during the war.

That priest would go onto to be named a saint in the Catholic church – St. Pio of Pietrelcina. And meeting him would have an impact on my father for the rest of his life...and on my family and me to this day.

* With the Sixth War Loan Drive, the United States Treasury Department offered what were known as defense bonds to raise money to support the war effort.

Chapter 2 – Some Art History

Arthur Haumesser and Family – Buffalo, NY, 1923

"Hey look! There's a house on fire!" shouted the red-headed girl from her desk near the classroom windows. The other students leapt from their seats to look out and see billows of black clouds hovering over nearby Columbus Avenue. Arthur joined the gawking crowd only to soon realize... it was his house!

Within moments, an older nun hurried into the seventh grade class and sent Arthur home. Running with all his might down Columbus, young Art's heart raced with fear. As he turned up the driveway, he saw the fire had been extinguished—it had burned the garage, not the house. His four-year-old brother, Robert, the youngest of the family, had been playing with matches.

When I was growing up, my father loved to tell that family tale, especially when his brother Bob was around to kid about the incident.

Arthur Joseph Haumesser was born in 1922 in Buffalo, New York, the second eldest son of his German immigrant father, Charles, and American-born mother, Anna. Despite family financial struggles, my dad often told stories of a pleasant childhood growing up in the roaring 1920s and the Great Depression of the 1930s. Holy Family, the grammar school and Catholic parish he attended, stood watch over his urban neighborhood known as South Buffalo.

The patriarch

I won't drag out the whole family history here, but want to briefly discuss my grandfather. Because his death represents a key moment in my father's war experience leading up to the meeting of Padre Pio.

Charles Martin Haumesser immigrated to America in 1901 at the age of 19 from the Alsace-Lorraine region of Germany. He came to Buffalo where he had family, and met Anna Mary Hartman. They married in 1912. Charles worked as a self-employed carpenter, taking on whatever work he could find to support their family of seven children. Buffalo was a growing city and there was plenty of work for a skilled carpenter in the early 1900s and 1920s.

Still, life was hard for Charles and Anna. A daughter, Leora, died at two years old of a childhood illness in 1929. The family struggled during the Great Depression like so many Americans. My father recalled walking with his mother and siblings along the railroad tracks that crossed Tifft Street, picking up lumps of coal that had fallen from passing trains. His mother would carry the found coal in her apron to use in the old kitchen stove back home.

During World War II, three of fours sons were serving in the military—my father in Italy; the oldest son, Carl, in Europe in the U.S. Army; and the second youngest, Norman, training stateside to ship out at some point with the U.S. Navy to Europe. Youngest son, Robert, was only nine when the Japanese attacked Pearl Harbor. Two older sisters, Virginia and Marie were either married or engaged to wed.

Anna Haumesser and children – L to R: Marie, Anna and Virginia,
Robert, Norman, Arthur and Carl. Post-war 1945

BIG BROTHER'S INFLUENCE

MY GRANDPARENTS WERE Catholic and my father was raised in the faith. But his own, deep faith was probably instilled more in high school than influenced by his parents or neighborhood parish. His older brother Carl had attended a college preparatory school in Buffalo, Canisius High School, run by the Jesuits, a Catholic religious order. Carl paid the tuition on his own, working after school at different jobs.

Nine years older than my father, Carl thought so much of Canisius High School that he paid for my father to attend the school, when it would have been impossible for his carpenter dad to afford the tuition. Carl would be an inspiration for my father during World War II as well.

The Jesuit influence was still fresh in Art's mind when he was drafted into the Army a couple of years after graduation. It was this faith that would ultimately connect him with Chaplain George Rice and the future Catholic saint.

CHAPTER 3 – MEETING RUTH

My mother, Ruth Haumesser – nee Butz – was born on November 25, 1923 in Buffalo, the eldest child and daughter of Charles and Bertha. While not wealthy, her father, also a German immigrant and a World War I U.S. Navy veteran, ran his own business selling barber and beauty supplies. The family enjoyed a middle class lifestyle. With a younger sister and brother, Ruth went to Catholic schools, singing in choirs and making lots of friends in her neighborhood known as the East Side of Buffalo.

Art had graduated from high school in 1940 and was attending Bryant & Stratton, a local two-year business college, when he first met my mother. She was a senior at an all-girls Catholic school called Sacred Heart Academy all the way across town in a northern part of the city.

The two had crossed paths at a couple of parties and at a roller skating rink. My father thought of Ruth as just a friend of Jean Marie's, part of a group of companions that included blond-haired Gordon Schilling, one of Art's best friends from high school. (Gordon would go on to join the Marines in World War II. He made it home safely, and Gordon and Art remained lifelong friends.)

Gordon Schilling, Jack Kager and Art – 1940

Time passed, and Art and Ruth ran into each other again in the spring of 1942. By summer, Art saw Ruth as more than just a friend of Jean Marie's. They began dating in July, spending time with what my mother described as a happy-go-lucky gang of friends. Art would ride the above-ground trolley cars from his home in South Buffalo to see Ruth across town. My mom used to say her mom and dad approved of Art because his family and her parents had mutual friends within Buffalo's large German American community.

The young couple spent the summer picnicking in the parks south of the city, going to movies, and keeping up with news of the war. But soon the shadows of Pearl Harbor caught up with them. Art was drafted toward the end of 1942.

CHAPTER 4 – IN THE AIR

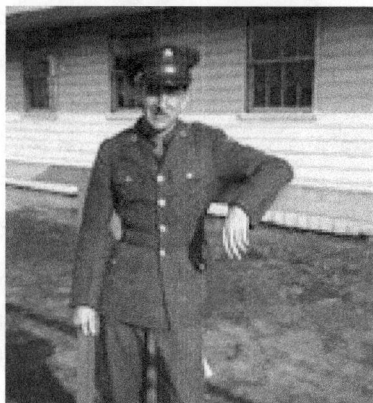

Art while training stateside – 1943

"I'M STILL HERE at Fort Niagara but not for long I hope. I have passed the exams for the Air Corps and the lieutenant signed our recommendations. We will probably go to Mitchel Field first for basic training, for everyone has to take some basic training whatever branch they may be in. Then will come intensive study and hard work. This will take about 36 weeks or almost nine months. Tomorrow it will be one week that I have been here and that's one week too much. This living out of a barracks bag and waiting in line in the cold to eat isn't very comfortable." – Art

My father received his induction notice in late 1942 and, in mid-January 1943, was sent to Fort Niagara in Niagara Falls, New York, the local barracks and training station for newly drafted soldiers. Fort Niagara was one of two induction centers in New York state during the war, the other located at Camp Upton on Long Island. Temporary training buildings, mess halls and barracks had been constructed at Fort Niagara which became my father's home away from nearby home for a few weeks.

Art joined other draftees in undergoing medical examinations, testing and other procedures meant to ensure the soldiers-to-be were fit for fighting in the war. He got a taste of Army life right away as the men were taught how to march, dress, and line up for inspection by snarling drill sergeants ready to assign KP duty for a soldier's slightest slip up.

Treatment of the soldiers at the induction centers was purposefully rough, as the U.S. military looked to identify strengths and weaknesses and assign men to various branches of the armed forces. Making matters worse, January at Fort Niagara was most often cold and miserable.

Originally built by the French in 1726 to protect their interests in colonial North America, the Fort sits on the eastern bank of the Niagara River where it flows into Lake Ontario. Winter winds screaming off the water across the open training grounds would have been brutally chilling to the marching soldiers. With his home in Buffalo just a 30-minute drive away, thoughts of going AWOL would have easily crossed Art's mind. But he stuck it out, buoyed by some good news.

The exams he mentioned in the letter made him eligible for the Air Force – then known as the Army Air Corps – a growing and important branch of America's military might. He would be leaving Fort Niagara to train as an Army Air Corps cadet. It would be the first leg of the journey that would lead to encounters with Padre Pio.

CHAPTER 5 – HOLDING PATTERN

"I'VE COME TO a detour on the road to becoming an air cadet. After almost three weeks of coughing and blowing, I finally convinced them I needed a nurse's care. The doctor who examined me here said that I had bronchitis, mid-way to pneumonia. I was the 22nd to be sent to the hospital from our barracks." – Art

From Fort Niagara, my father was sent to Mitchel Field on Long Island in the third week of January. By the first week of February he was in the barracks hospital with pneumonia. It likely started in the cold winter weather at Fort Niagara. He would spend the next 53 days in Santini Hospital at Mitchel Field.

The pneumonia worsened and he became so critically ill, his mother took a train from Buffalo to come see him. There was not not enough money for both parents to afford the train, so Art's mother traveled the 14+ hours by herself.

"Yesterday was the happiest day I've spent here in the hospital. In the morning, I got a letter from my mother saying she would be down to see me Sunday or Monday. So Sunday afternoon she walks in! She expected the letter to get here on Saturday but she didn't consider the Army postal service. It was a wonderful feeling to see her come around the corner. She stayed until about five and left to visit a cousin in Paterson, New Jersey and then went home Monday from there." – Art

It was nearing the end of February and satisfied her son was going to be okay, my grandmother returned home. My father slowly recovered and by the end of March he was released from the hospital and returned to the unit to which he had been assigned at Mitchel Field.

Later in life, if you asked my father what basic training was like during the war, he'd laugh and reply, "I don't know. I missed most of it because I was in the hospital for nearly two months."

While he missed most of the physical aspects of basic training, Art returned to air cadet training, eventually being transferred in April to Maxwell Field in Montgomery, Alabama where he would attend pre-flight school. He studied math and algebra, aircraft recognition, Morse code and signal communications among many other subjects. In addition, the soldiers marched and drilled every day under strict supervision.

"It's really miserable here; in fact, it is intended to be miserable to weed out those who have no real feeling for flying. We are under direct supervision of the upperclassmen who really do supervise. Everything from fingernails to quarters are criticized by them and if they find anything wrong, we get 'gigged'. Gigs are demerits and if one gets more than five in one week, he walks a tour which is just walking around and around a rectangular area.

"There are rules and regulations galore. One of the hardest things to do is eating mess. That sounds strange but if you had to do it the way we have to, you'd know why. We have to sit at strict attention, shoulders back, head erect. The eyes must be kept on the plate and with head erect, it's not easy. One hardly ever sees what one is eating. I'd tell you more, but I haven't much more time." – Art

In another letter from Maxwell Field, Art further described more discomfort in the heat of the Alabama spring.

"This parade I mentioned occurs about 3 or 4 times per week. In every Army post at 5:30 in the afternoon, a ceremony called retreat is held. This is when they take down the flag for the day. On parade, the squadrons from the whole field mass on the field for this ceremony. About all we do is march up there and stand at attention under a broiling sun for about a half an hour. The sweat just pours down your face, nearly driving one crazy for you can't raise a hand to wipe it off." – Art

The classroom studies continued, including physics and aeronautics, as did Art's dream of becoming a pilot.

"We had a very enjoyable and thrilling air show here yesterday. Four pilots, just returned from Alaska, put on a demonstration in P-51 Mustangs. They'd come flying across the field at about 250 or 300 miles per hour, about 15 to 25 feet off the ground. Those are beautiful ships and I'd certainly like to handle one some day."– Art

By the end of June, my father had finished pre-flight school and he would move on to primary flight training at Souther Field in Americus, Georgia.

Chapter 6 – Taking off

Art in 1986 next to Stearman training biplane

"At this writing I have about 1-1/2 hours in the air. Today was my second day up and already I feel like a veteran for things are done so fast. We got off all right, the instructor doing this, though. After gaining some altitude he demonstrated simple right and left turns. Then came the moment of moments. The instructor says through the tube, 'Take over!' By a system of prearranged hand signals he had me do left and right turns. I don't know how well I did, but I'm still alive. One thing about the instructors – they're not easy on us. If we do something wrong, they yell their heads off at us. If you can take it okay after a barrage from them, you won't make the same mistake again very easily." – Art

At Souther Field, my father joined more than 600 cadets vying to become pilots. They learned to fly in Boeing Stearman biplanes, often called P-17s, in which the instructor sat behind the cadet. Primary flying school included more classroom study in addition to hours up in the air. It was an anxious time.

"As far as instruction goes, I'm rather worried. For the last two days, I have practiced landings and take-offs and if they don't improve soon, it will be too bad. I'm once more a bouncing baby if my landings are any indication. I seem to be gliding in so nicely when all of the sudden the ground comes up and smacks me sending me back into the ozone. When you consider that the ship comes in at better than 70 miles an hour, you can realize what it's like." – Art

Art continued to fly through the month of July 1943 and his anxiety was relieved somewhat by a visit from his big brother, Carl.

"My brother Carl is coming over from Fort Benning Saturday night to see me and I hope nothing interferes. I haven't seen him since last November and it will be quite a reunion. However, I wish I could see him next Monday at Benning. That's when he will graduate from OCS* and receive his commission as a second lieutenant." – Art

Fort Benning was a little more than an hour's drive from Souther Field and Carl would be able to spend a good portion of the weekend with him. Unfortunately, whatever encouragement big brother might bring to support the young cadet would be short-lived.

*Officer Candidate School

Chapter 7 – Coming down

"This is one of the hardest letters I have ever had to write. I don't know just how to tell you. Perhaps you have heard the sad tidings from my mother or sister. However, here goes. I regret to inform you that Air Cadet A.J. Haumesser has been eliminated from further flight training. Last Tuesday, I failed an Army check ride and I am no longer flying.

"Whatever gave me the idea that I could fly, I don't know. I should have realized in the beginning that such things were not meant for me. As I told Mom, I guess the main reason for my joining this outfit was to prove to some people and more so to myself that I could do something that was considered better than average; that I was equal with fellows like those back in high school who got all the recognition while I remained in the background.

"The worst part is that I have failed you and disappointed you, Ruth, and all my folks back home. I hope, though, that this doesn't change your opinion of me in any way." – Art

In August, Art washed out as a pilot. He often spoke of how he scraped the wing of the Stearman biplane along the runway during his last landing and that was it. He failed primary school. No matter how many times I heard him tell that story, I could always sense the profound disappointment in his voice, even 60 years later. I think it was a "could've been" experience for him that he played over and over in his head the rest of his life.

He signed off the letter to my mother as "Art (ex-pilot)" underlining his dejection. Unfortunately, the letters from my mother responding to my father during this time period are missing. My guess is my father brought them home to Buffalo during his final furlough and left them in the family home on Columbus Avenue. They were not among the letters saved by my father in the old cardboard box.

Nonetheless, I would venture to guess that my father's washout of pilot school didn't change my mother's opinion of him. She was not one to be impressed by status. She simply loved Art for who he was and it would not matter to her if he became a pilot or not. She just wanted him to return home to her safely.

Now, Art would now go before an Army Air Corps board made up of officers at Souther Field who would decide his fate. He found hope in the board's decision.

"Down again up again! My days as a pilot may be over, but I'm still going to fly. This morning I was informed that I am leaving tomorrow at 4 AM for navigation school, Selman Field, Monroe, Louisiana. I still get a commission and a pair of wings even though I won't fly my own ship. I was really lucky to get it I think for there are four of us going there. The rest of those eliminated – about 45 – are going to Biloxi as privates while I'll still be an air cadet. Once more I can say, 'Keep 'em Flying!'" – Art

Art joined Class 43-20 at the Army Air Forces Navigator School in Monroe, Louisiana in early September. There was more classroom training on traditional navigation tools such as maps and compasses as well as the latest technology for the times such as radio beacons. The anxiety Art felt in pilot school had lessened, yet navigation school proved challenging with lots more study. By the late fall of 1943, after many weeks of training, he wrote to my mother with more bad news.

Chapter 8 – Losing his way

"I wish I didn't have to write this letter or at least what's in it. I don't know how to tell you this because – at least I would like to think – you were so proud of me and had such faith in me being in the cadets and trying for a commission. It's doubly disheartening coming after my washout from pilot training. You've undoubtedly guessed what I am attempting to say… that I've been eliminated from navigation school.

"As for what lies ahead, it may not be too bad. The board with which I met this morning said there were four openings in the Air Force for me now; radio operator, radio operator mechanic, mechanic and armorer. I chose radio operator for I know a little bit about it and have always been interested in it.

"I hope you're not too disappointed in me, Ruth, but I promise you that whatever I do next will receive my best effort." – Art

Art didn't make the grade in navigation school but the Air Force still had plans for him. My father would spend the next nine months or so training to be a radio operator. This time he passed all the requirements and was assigned to train with a B-17 Flying Fortress crew, going from Scott Field in Illinois to Yuma, Arizona and then to Alexandria, Virginia.

I have some of the books and tests he took, and while primitive by today's technology, the radio training was very technical. Complicated stuff to master, for sure, thus the long period of training. He wouldn't be a pilot or a navigator, or an officer for that matter, but he would still get to fly. And it would be life defining.

CHAPTER 9 – THE LONG GOOD-BYE

The last photo taken of Arthur with his father – 1944

My FATHER CAME home one last time on furlough, for about a week in the summer of 1944, before leaving on the next round of assignments that would eventually take him overseas. Looking at the old photos, I can imagine the family gathering to say good-bye to Art on a warm June week-end in Buffalo, when summer's early sway helped them forget for a moment why they had gathered.

A pretty good crowd would have been there – Art's youngest brother and his sisters; uncles, aunts and cousins; maybe even a few neighborhood friends. Photos were taken in the yard. A Sunday dinner was enjoyed. My grandmother's apron would be wet from doing the dishes – and perhaps some tears – when everyone had left.

No one would have said it, but the family, even with the most hopeful of hearts, had to wonder if this might be the last time they saw Art. It would be the last time Art saw his father.

Chapter 10 – Last stop, Lincoln

"A LONG TIME ago, when you first asked me to come down if and when you wouldn't be able to come home, I decided I'd go see you even if it was California. I've been talking with your mother and we have made a lot of plans and all those plans center on you, A.J. I can hardly wait! Who knows where it will be, Lincoln or Kearney, Nebraska, or maybe Topeka, Kansas. But any place will do as long as you're in it. Now I can really begin to sing my theme song again – I'll Be Seeing You – and mean it!" – Ruth

After my dad's June furlough, my mother traveled by train with her future mother-in-law to visit him at his final stateside assignment in Lincoln, Nebraska. They spent about a week visiting Lincoln, going out to eat, and seeing the latest movies, Ruth always under the watchful eye of Art's mother.

My father and mother would spend Sunday, October 15, 1944 together

before he left on his 7,000-mile journey into war. He gave her his Canisius High School ring with a promise that he would have a real engagement ring for her when he returned.

"Say, A.J., how does that ring finger of yours feel? Half-dressed? Never fear, I'm taking good care of your ring. I've got a couple of feet of string wrapped around it until I can get a guard for it. Wouldn't want to lose it you know. It's too precious and it means too much to me." – Ruth

I can see my father kissing my mother good-bye that last day, his pride as an airman masking his angst about leaving. They would not see each other for nearly another year. The letters – correspondence that began during my father's stateside training – kept them connected through the rest of the war.

"I hope I never again have to have that awful feeling of loneliness I felt when I saw you walking away from us. I know it must have been doubly hard for you. Your mother and I had each other for consolation, but you were alone." – Ruth

My father shared Ruth's sentiment.

"It was like a dream, knowing that it couldn't last forever and yet enjoying every minute of it. When you finally had to leave it was as if I had awakened and that terrible loneliness just spread right over me again." – Art

Art and Ruth – 1944

THE FINAL CREW

THE 10-MAN CREW formed in Lincoln would stay together throughout most of the war, representing the United States from coast to coast – New York to California – and north to south – Minneapolis to Alabama. For most, it was the first time they ever met and spent so much time with anyone outside of their home towns. Now, they were about to enter another world together.

The crew left Lincoln on October 17 and arrived in Italy on October 30, after a multi-stop trip involving 42 hours of flying. The trip included a six-day layover in Newfoundland and a three-day layover in Marrakesh, Morocco. Incredibly, my father flew right over his neighborhood at the start of the trip.

"Remember I said I'd fly over Buffalo? Well, that Tuesday morning at exactly five after ten, I was just 9,000 feet from home. I was right up in the nose with a pair of binoculars picking out 20 Columbus, 25 Langmeyer and other places. From New Hampshire we went to Newfoundland; then the long haul across the Atlantic to the Azores. Except for one bad storm, we did all right. We then went to French Morocco in Africa; then to Tunis. The last leg you know of." – Art

My mother knew Art was headed to the Mediterranean theater, but not a specific town or country. Her long wait had begun.

"It's been a week today since I last saw you and it seems like a year. Last Sunday night I at least knew where you were; this Sunday I can't be certain just where you are. Perhaps I shouldn't keep writing things like this, it might make you feel worse. But it helps a lot to speak what's in my heart and I know you understand." – Ruth

The crew – as formed in Lincoln, Nebraska, 1944
Left to Right Front Row: Pilot – Lt. William Connor from San Francisco; Co-Pilot – Lt. William Deane from Minneapolis; Navigator – Lt. John Campbell from Massachusetts; Bombardier – Lt. Phillips from Minnesota. Back Row: Upper Turret – Ernest Conrad from Brooklyn, New York; Radio Operator – Arthur Haumesser from Buffalo; Right Waist Gunner – Robert Burns from New Jersey; Ball Turret – Frank DeSilvey from Mobile, Alabama; Tail Gunner – Charles Dawson from Denver, Colorado; Left Waist Gunner – John Cummins from Clinton, Arkansas.

CHAPTER 11 – FLYBOYS IN FOGGIA

"WHEN WE ARRIVED here, they gave us a tent, one of those large pyramidal types, and a few cots. It's up to us to fix it up any way we wish. So today we got a load of bricks and put in a floor. They promised us electricity but so far we've had to use candles. They even gave us a recreation kit containing a football, baseballs, checkerboard, games, etc. I did get another watch and also a swell pair of sunglasses." – Art

My father and his crew were stationed at Celone Airfield, about six miles north of Foggia, Italy. Foggia had been heavily bombed by the Allies because it held important airfields and marshalling yards for the Nazis. The city was briefly occupied by German troops in 1943, but as Allied soldiers advanced in September, the occupiers abandoned the area. By October, British troops had successfully taken over the city and Allied air fields were built around Foggia.

Art and the crew were part of the 463rd Bomb Group made up of four squadrons – the 772nd, 773rd, 774th and 775th. The 463rd flew out of Celone to attack German targets such as marshalling yards, oil refineries, and aircraft factories in Italy, Germany, Austria, and other territories held by the Nazis. My father's crew was in the 774th Squadron and the majority of their missions were over Germany and Italy.

Manning the radio

ONE OF 10 CREWMEN on the B-17, Art was a radio operator and gunner. The radio system on a B-17 provided for communications between crew members within the ship, as well as between the airplane and ground stations and other airplanes.

The radio operator monitored the bomb group frequencies during each mission to keep pace with any changes to the flight plan. If the lead plane decided to makes changes, the radio operator passed the information on to the pilot.

The radio man also had a clear view of the bomb bay and would check the area for damage or a hung bomb when the aircraft flew off of the target. My dad told the story of a bomb that got hung up on the rack during one mission and how he had to quickly kick the oversized shell to disengage it while they were over a large field. He'd laugh and say he hoped he hadn't scared some poor cow.

Another radio operator in the 463ʳᵈ Bomb Group, in the 772ⁿᵈ Squadron, was Norman Lear from New Haven, Connecticut. Lear would survive the war and go on to fame and fortune in the 1970s as a writer and producer of such groundbreaking television comedies as *All in the Family*, *Sanford and Sons*, *The Jeffersons* and *One Day at a Time*. I don't recall my father ever mentioning Lear, but he certainly would have known him in the 463ʳᵈ, as a fellow radio operator on the same base. I do know my father was not a fan of *All in the Family*.

Taking aim

MY FATHER WAS also a gunner, firing, when necessary, a .50 caliber machine gun located in the ceiling that swung out a top window facing the rear of the aircraft. A Plexiglass cover protected the gunner from cold and wind. The B-17G – the version the 774ᵗʰ would have flown – had thirteen .50 caliber guns throughout the ship, living up to the bomber's nickname, the Flying Fortress.

Art never spoke of firing the guns on missions, but he certainly would have. In one letter home, he describes a Catholic group he belonged to on base called Gunners for Mary. That's right, Gunners for Mary. The name certainly wouldn't fly today, but it was a serious group of Catholic men who held prayer services to honor Mary, the mother of Jesus Christ.

I wonder what it was like for my father. Holding rosary beads one day and firing a gun at the enemy the next. The sacred and the profane. But I am sure he found comfort in the group and carried that strengthened faith with him on each mission.

Years later, when my father lay dying in Buffalo's Veteran's Administration (VA) hospital, he said something to my brother and me that suggests he would have felt terrible about shooting a person in battle. Perhaps it is why he never spoke of firing his gun. That is covered in a later chapter.

Chapter 12 – Bombs away

"There were these huge aerial cameras in the floor of the radio compartment in the B-17. I was assigned to take bomb strike photos. You had to open up a floor board to access the cameras which let in a cold blast of air, right in your face as you tried to take the photos. One mission, I decided to remain in my radio operator's seat, and planting my warm boot on top of the camera, took the photos with my feet. The next morning at base, lo and behold, there was an announcement on the bulletin board that said Sergeant Arthur Haumesser has taken some great bomb strike photos!" – Art

That was one of the lighter war tales my dad often told with a laugh. But I never really heard him say much about the bad stuff. And having completed 30 bombing missions, he certainly saw some bad stuff. There's a famous raid on Berlin detailed in later chapters that serves as a prime example.

Just a week before his dad died in November 1944, my father had flown his first mission, the bombing of a German marshalling yard in Salzburg, Austria. All 31 planes on the mission returned safely after being in the air for over seven hours.

That is seven hours in what is essentially a tin can with powerful motors, flying over German territory in dreaded anticipation of enemy defenders aiming to blow the tin can out of the sky. My father described the mission.

"Well, honey, I've had my so-called baptism by fire, and it wasn't half, no, not one quarter as bad as you might think. I can't tell you where we went or when, but there are a few incidents I'll tell you of. We nearly had a couple of casualties. Frank became air sick and had trouble with his oxygen and so passed out for a while. After Bob and I had fixed him up, everything was okay for a while. Then I happened to look up toward the nose and there was Ernie stretched out cold. His hose became disconnected while trying to put on his flak suit. It was really a close call for him, for at 30,000 feet lack of oxygen is a serious thing.

"Another incident, if I may call it that, was the cold. It was 50 degrees below zero centigrade up there today and changed into Fahrenheit, it's even more. Ordinarily, that wouldn't have been so bad since we have electrically heated suits to wear. But mine wasn't working and I darn near froze up solid. The suits are nice, though (when they work). There's a pair of pants that come way up to your chest; then, plugged into that is a jacket, into which you plug a pair of gloves. Also included is a pair of slippers plugged into the pants." – Art

My father's letter may not have been all that calming for my mother, especially calling it his baptism by fire. It probably made her worry more as she noted in a response.

"So you've flown your first mission. And you say it wasn't half bad. Oh, that's just like you trying to make light of something, just to keep me from worrying, and I love you for it!" – Ruth

Art and his fellow crew members would certainly have returned to their air base in high spirits, celebrating their inaugural success. They were not so lucky the next time.

Four days later, the crew went up on a similar mission over Innsbruck,

Austria. The formation of B-17s was met by thick, black clouds of heavy flak shot by German anti-aircraft guns down below.

German flak consisted of an explosive shell with metal fragment shards, ball bearings or nail-like objects that would all be propelled by the blast of the shell. Crew members wore flak jackets to protect themselves from flak pieces that would ricochet inside the cabin after tearing through the plane's thin aluminum fuselage.

On the Innsbruck mission, a plane carrying the commanding officer of the 774th squadron, Major Joseph Compton, and his crew was hit and it spiraled toward the ground. Other crews looked for parachutes as the ship dropped, but there were none reported. The reality of the air war must hit my father like the explosive bombs they dropped.

Back at the base, 10 empty beds in the 774th tents and open seats in the mess hall served to remind them of the loss. And there was much more to come.

It was after those first two missions in November that Arthur learned about his father's death from the base chaplain. A young soldier surrounded in sadness, contemplating the loss of his father – who he fondly remembered as a "swell" dad – only to have to suck it up for the next mission.

Chapter 13 – The accident

Norm, Anna, Charles and Carl Haumesser – 1944

"THIS LETTER IS going to be short for there isn't much I can say. This morning, the chaplain, Father Rice, told me that my father had died a week ago. I'm just now beginning to believe it after spending a day thinking about it. His absence from my daily routine of things for such a long time makes it hard for me to realize he is gone. Perhaps when I get home again, amid those familiar surroundings, I'll really miss him for the first time." – Art

Charles Haumesser was a carpenter, a skill he had picked up working on family farms in Holtzwihr, Alsace-Lorraine, an area on the border of Germany and France. He had managed to make a living at it when he came to Buffalo as a young man.

Stories vary on where Charles was headed the morning of November 18, 1944 when he was hit by the car. Small in stature but fit from the labors of his trade, he liked to take walks in the South Buffalo neighborhood. He may have been headed to a job or a nearby relative's house. I recently visited Columbus Avenue, the street on which he lived, and envisioned my grandfather strolling passed densely packed, well-kept homes shaded by a canopy of large, beautiful elm trees. The trees are long gone and the houses show their age, but I felt the sense of community my grandfather would have shared with his neighbors, mostly working-class Irish- and German-American families.

It was around 7 AM on a Saturday when Charles was struck by a speeding car at McKinley Parkway and Tifft Street. The car never stopped. He was unconscious when an ambulance took him to nearby Mercy Hospital where he held on until Monday night before slipping away from his injuries. He was 62.

It was three days before Thanksgiving, but there was not a lot for which to be thankful. My grandmother was just 52, left alone to raise young Bob, with her three other sons fighting in the war.

"This is supposed to be quite a holiday, isn't it? I'm afraid it didn't seem much like one to you over there or to us at home either. But we must think of all the blessings we do have and be grateful for them. I'll close now for there is a big day ahead tomorrow. Please dear, take care of yourself, won't you? I'll worry about you more than ever now. Does it help any to know that I love you very much? I hope so." – Ruth

My grandfather's funeral was held the Friday after Thanksgiving.

"My heart is heavy tonight and of course you know the reason why. Your mother held up, marvelously, Art. It's as if she were supported by some inner strength which none of us can see. That's what prayer does for one." – Ruth

I wish I had known my grandfather and wonder what it was like for him, coming to America from Germany, and then to have three of his sons in a war against his homeland. Whatever the reason for leaving home, Charles would have been proud of his boys in World War II, and equally proud to have been an American citizen.

My grandfather's death was the catalyst that led my father to his first meeting with Padre Pio. Given Art's strong Catholic faith, it is likely Father Rice would have taken him with other soldiers to meet the Italian priest at some point, even if my grandfather had not been killed.

But the chaplain's compassion and concern for the emotionally wounded soldier gave my father an extraordinary experience to meet Padre Pio one on one.

CHAPTER 14 – MEETING THE MYSTIC

"FATHER RICE HAS been swell to me. He invited me to drive up to a place in the mountains called San Giovanni Rotondo. There lives in a monastery there a very holy and sainted priest, Padre Pio, who, it has been acknowledged, has performed numerous miracles. We met him and kissed his hands which bear the marks of the nails of the cross. We were not able to converse with him, although Father Rice could by the use of Latin. It was a wonderful experience and one which I will never forget." – Art

My father first met Padre Pio – Saint Pio of Pietrelcina – when Father Rice took the airman to visit the priest in November 1944. Recognizing Art's deep faith and his sorrow in losing his dad, the chaplain took him under his wing, knowing a visit to Padre Pio would mean a lot to the Catholic soldier. The chaplain and my father drove in an Army jeep to a monastery in the mountains, San Giovanni Rotondo, about 25 miles away from Foggia. My father described the dirt roads up the mountain as winding and treacherous. It was another leg of a life-altering journey for Art.

By this time, San Giovanni and surrounding areas had been liberated from the German army and word of a very holy man with intense spirituality began to spread among the Allied troops. Padre Pio had the stigmata – he bore the wounds of the crucified Jesus Christ in his hands and feet, and as my father had recounted in his letter, meeting the priest was an experience he would never forget.

THE STIGMATA

COUNTLESS BOOKS AND articles have been written about St. Pio and he is often regarded as the greatest mystic of the twentieth century. Likewise, countless writers have accused Padre Pio of being a fraud, saying the wounds were self-inflicted or due to some hysteria suffered by the priest.

The stigmata first appeared on Padre Pio in 1918 and remained with him the rest of his life. The wounds never healed and he wore fingerless gloves to cover his hands. During the 1920s and 1930s, word spread of the holy man, including stories of miracles, and the faithful began to flock to the monastery in San Giovanni.

Local church leaders at the time thought the Capuchin order of priests was using Padre Pio for their own financial gain. The Vatican performed numerous investigations, and while there was never any conclusive evidence of fraud, Padre Pio was banned from saying Mass in public, hearing confessions, and even answering letters sent to him by believers.

Pope Pius XI kept these bans in place until the mid 1930s, when he lifted them saying he may have been misinformed about the priest. The pope's successor, Pope Pius XII – who my father also met during the war – began to encourage people to visit Padre Pio, finding the priest to be a humble, faithful man who had nothing to gain from fakery.

SPIRITUAL CHILDREN

AS STORIES OF Padre Pio continued to be told among the soldiers in World War II, their visits were warmly welcomed by the Capuchin priest. He already had a strong affinity for America.

Padre Pio was born Francesco Forgione in southern Italy in 1887, part of a family of humble, hardworking farmers. The priest's father had come to America in 1899 to earn money so that Padre Pio could finish his education and enter into the Capuchin friary in San Giovanni. The elder Forgione worked on a farm in Pennsylvania where some relatives lived – near New Castle and each week he sent money back home to Italy.

During the war, as American soldiers bravely stood up to the evil of Hitler, they also discovered a calm peace with Padre Pio. He referred to the soldiers who visited as his American spiritual children. Encountering this pious, future saint while fighting a maniacal monster across the border in Germany most certainly steeled my father's faith and gave him the perseverance to carry on with the fight.

Like my father, so many soldiers wrote home with their stories of the monk, and Padre Pio began to gain notoriety around the United States and the world.

"I was talking to your mother today. She told me of the monastery you visited there in Italy. That must have been a very beautiful place from your description. It must have been quite an experience to see that old priest."
– Ruth

Today's Catholic Church has no proven explanation of the stigmata and recognizes the phenomenon as a miracle and a mystery. Nonetheless – as my father would often explain in his later years – St. Pio promotes the example of Christ to the faithful, thus, no matter the evidence or scientific conclusions, he is in keeping with the teachings of the church. Compassion. Humility. Love.

Skeptics, of course, continue to doubt. Stigmata is not easy to accept, especially for non-Catholics. As for me, I have to put myself in the category of believers in St. Pio. My father, of course, is the biggest influence. How can I doubt my own dad? Then, reading his letters revealed the numerous times he went to see Padre Pio and detailed what he witnessed during those visits. My belief has been sharpened by Art's very own words in his letters.

Chapter 15 – A familiar face

Clipping from Buffalo newspaper

"Here's an item for the papers. 'Brothers reunited in Italy.' Last Saturday morning I returned from chow and started to enter the tent when there he stood. You could have knocked me over with a you know what. He stayed all day Saturday then had to leave Sunday morning. We tried to find him a ride on a plane but the weather kept all flying to a minimum." – Art

Art loved his big brother, Carl, and it was a big deal to connect with him during the war. It was in early December, just a couple of weeks after their father's passing that Carl arrived at Art's air base. Next to the first Padre Pio visit, there could have been no greater comfort for my father than to see his brother, sharing in their grief.

Like my father, Carl was unable to return to Buffalo for the funeral. Carl served as a 1st Lieutenant and intelligence officer with the 91st Infantry Division and was stationed throughout Europe including Italy where he was when his father died.

My dad always talked about that visit, brimming with younger sibling pride even in his later years. He would recall how Carl and he went in to the officer's club on base, even though my father was an enlisted man. When the catcalls started about a mere sergeant being in the club, Carl barked back at them, "He's with me!" The room quieted in an instant according to my father.

Chapter 16 – Choir boys

Art with the choir, second from right in front row.

"Tonight the choir is heading to Padre Pio's again and after I finish this letter, I'll be going. We had intended to sing a missa cantata* for Padre Pio's mass but we found out it won't be a high mass. So we will just sing a few hymns for him. I'll remember you at Padre Pio's mass tomorrow morning." – Art

When the airmen of the 463rd Bomb Group weren't sailing through the clouds during missions of war, a small group of them were raising their voices to the heavens in a Catholic choir.

Chaplain George Rice formed the choir as another small comfort – maybe even a distraction – for soldiers of faith like my father. Between missions, there were often stretches of boredom, and the chaplain held choir practices to occupy the down time and strengthen their Catholic faith.

As he did with Art, Father Rice had taken numerous American soldiers to visit Padre Pio and the chaplain must have gotten to know the future saint quite well. Because before long, the voices of these young American soldiers filled the church at San Giovanni Rotondo, singing at masses on several occasions for Padre Pio.

Members of the choir with Padre Pio – L to R: Gerald Adamic, Howard Crimmins, Arthur Haumesser, John McCormack, Padre Pio, seated, John Quinn, unidentified, Ernest Conrad, and last one unidentified

Members of choir – determined from names found on the back of old photographs – included John Quinn and Fred Specht, both from Chicago; Howard Crimmins from Cuba City, Wisconsin; John Bandi from Pittsburgh; Jim Peabody from Stonington, Illinois; Ernie Conrad from Brooklyn; and of course, my father from Buffalo. Ernie spoke some Italian which helped in communicating with the locals on their travels to San Giovanni.

Gerald Adamic was an Army photographer who traveled and sang with the choir on a couple of occasions. He took numerous photos at San Giovanni Rotondo that appear in the 463rd year book and were once submitted to Life Magazine for story consideration during the war.

Choir members in front of the monastery, 1945

"I just spent two of the most wonderful days I'll ever spend in Italy. Let me start at the beginning.

"Wednesday morning, Father Rice obtained a truck to take the members of the choir and a few others up to San Giovanni where is the monastery in which Padre Pio lives. You'll remember I told you of a previous visit up there.

"We left about noon and arrived an hour and a half later covered with dust after a long ride up those winding, tortuous mountain roads. We then looked up this Italian count who lives up there. He was educated in England and speaks perfect English, quite a character. We went to the monastery and met Padre Pio for a few moments, his time being very limited. The rest of the afternoon we spent looking around the town.

"Next morning, bright and early, we were up at five. Then we went to Padre Pio's mass at six. I wish you could have seen that mass. It was a regular low mass but it took him one hour and fifteen minutes to say it; that's excluding distribution of communion. He is in constant pain from the wounds and it takes quite an effort for him to genuflect.

"At mass is the only time he doesn't wear the small gloves over his hands and the blood runs from these wounds. He bears the wounds in his side and feet also and the blood from his side has been examined by doctors who say it contains water just as that from Christ's side. Other wounds and cuts heal naturally but these do not. We were privileged to hear the mass up at the altar along with the blind and sick who were there.

"There was one blind man who also stayed at the inn who has been promised his sight by Padre Pio when his wife has a child. The fellow's faith is unshakeable and he is very happy since his wife expects the baby within the next few days." – Art

In a letter from January of 1945 my father notes that the choir was preparing to sing High Mass at Padre Pio's on the anniversary of his joining the order. Being in the choir gave my father a ringside seat at the masses, as the choir often stood to the right of the altar. That is where my father witnessed Padre Pio grimacing and groaning, as the slightest movement during mass caused great pain in his wounded hands.

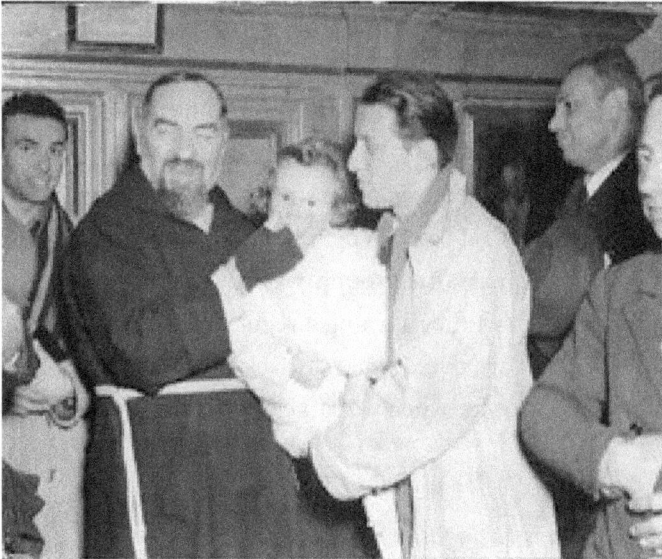

"Today has been a very wonderful day. Why? Well I just returned from another trip to Padre Pio's. We left about eight o'clock last night and after the long, rough ride up there, we were ready for bed immediately upon

arrival. We had breakfast in the morning and proceeded to the monastery.

"We had our misgivings about it because there were only five of the choir present, but it turned out pretty well according to what they said. I think their opinion of our choir was bettered a lot by Mac's singing of the 'Ave Maria'. He really has a wonderful voice.

"Well, mass was over about eleven-fifteen. Padre Pio said the mass, and it being a Solemn High Mass, our own Father Rice assisted. After mass, we went back into the sacristy (everyone goes back there; all the men that is, for women aren't allowed there or in the monastery) to kiss the wounds in his hands.

"There was a fellow back there with a child about a year and a half old, one of the prettiest children I've seen around here. All of us thought sure it was a girl but we should have known for what I said above and as we found out later that it was a boy. The reason I mention it is because a fellow with us who is a photographer got a swell picture of Padre Pio and the child. I'll send you one when I get a print." – Art

More than anything else, his first-hand experiences made my father a firm believer in the sanctity of Padre Pio. "People can say what they want, but I saw Padre Pio with my own two eyes, and he wasn't faking," my dad would emphatically tell us.

"The trip to Padre Pio passed quite successfully, although for a while we thought we might not get back. When we got up at five yesterday morning to go to Padre Pio's mass, the ground was covered with several inches of snow and for the rest of the morning a regular blizzard raged outdoors so that we didn't think we could make it back down the mountain. But we made it. It was strange for when we came back down here there was hardly any snow." – Art

Missa cantata is Latin for "sung mass".

CHAPTER 17 – L'AMERICANA MARY PYLE

Art on Mary Pyle's right, in her kitchen in San Giovanni

"I DON'T THINK I've mentioned her before, but living up there is a woman, Miss Mary Pyle, of New York City. She came here a number of years ago to visit the place and has never left it, simply to be near Padre Pio. She was telling us of many of the miracles which he has performed. She was telling us of a number of romances which he has helped along, too, and I couldn't help but think of us. Ruth, I'm absolutely sure that if you said a few prayers to him, you would be heard.

"Mary Pyle told us of one girl to whom Padre Pio appeared in a dream (she had never seen him before and did not know him) and told her that she would meet a man soon whom she would marry and who would be the right one for her. Later on, she met this man and after becoming engaged told him of her dream. Whereupon, the man showed her a picture of Padre Pio and asked if that were he. She answered yes." – Art

The mystery and magnetism of Padre Pio may best be reflected in the example of Mary Pyle, an American-born woman who dedicated her life to the future saint, serving as his right hand person until his death in 1968. As my father and the choir also had several visits with Mary, she would have bolstered his belief in Padre Pio.

Mary – baptized in the Presbyterian church as Adelia – was from a very wealthy New York City family. She was well-educated and spoke five languages. In her twenties, Mary traveled the world with Maria Montessori, the famous educator and founder of the Montessori schools. Mary would translate the lectures Montessori gave across Europe on her innovative approaches to education.

When they arrived in Italy, Mary paid a visit to Padre Pio, having heard of the mystic from the locals near San Giovanni. After meeting Padre Pio, Mary returned to Maria Montessori and told her she would no longer be traveling on the lecture tour. She was staying in San Giovanni to be near Padre Pio. Mary's parents disapproved of her decision and soon cut off any financial support.

Later on, when the parents visited Mary and met Padre Pio themselves, they said they understood, and reinstated their support. Mary used that money to help build an inn for the growing number of visitors Padre Pio was attracting.

There is currently a movement underway among Catholics to begin the canonization process for Mary Pyle based on her devotion to Padre Pio.

"I just got some photos of the choir taken the last time at San Giovanni. There's one of us all sitting around the table in Mary Pyle's house* having the usual cup of coffee she always serves. It is exceptionally good!" – Art

*A reference to the photo included in this chapter

Chapter 18 – War worry

"I HOPE EVERYTHING is going along all right over there. I haven't had any mail at all this week from you. Please don't think I'm complaining – I'm not. It's just that I can't help worrying a little bit. I don't have to tell you how it feels when you don't get any mail. Especially from my one and only." – Ruth

It was a winter to remember. In mid December of 1944, a big snow storm added to the frayed nerves of Art's fiancé and family back home in Buffalo. Transportation came to a halt. Even the railroads shut down, closing vital supply lines for the war effort as companies such as Bell Aircraft and Curtiss Wright in Buffalo produced significant materials for the war.

Bell Aircraft employed about 28,000 people in the Buffalo area during the war, producing nearly 10,000 of its renowned P-39 Airacobra planes, one of the principal American fighters in service when the United States entered the conflict.

The Bell plant near Buffalo also produced over 3,300 P-63 Kingcobra fighters, the majority of which were delivered to the Soviet Union under President Roosevelt's Lend-Lease program with U.S. Allies.

During the war, Curtiss-Wright operated two plants in the Buffalo area – the first at Kenmore Avenue and Vulcan Street in Tonawanda, and a 1.8 million square foot manufacturing facility near the Buffalo Niagara Airport. By 1943 there were more than 40,000 employees (a high percentage being women) producing more than 13,000 P-40 Warhawk airplanes used by most of the Allied powers throughout the war.

With so many men fighting in the war, and so many people working in local factories, the city faced a shortage of labor to plow streets and remove snow. Side streets were impassable. People had to walk wherever they wanted to go. My mother eventually had to stay home for a day or two from her job at the Iroquois Gas Company.

"The wind is howling like mad outside. It was terrible downtown this afternoon. I had all to do to keep my balance, that wind was so strong. You know how windy it always is on Church Street. They usually have ropes in front of the Telephone Building during those terrible winter wind storms." – Ruth

Stuck inside, people in Buffalo huddled around their radios for war news. They were able to learn what was going on in the war from newsmen stationed at the various fronts and other reports from the War Department.

Certainly, there was propaganda for the war effort, but for the most part, broadcasts were truthful and informative. Battles were won and lost. Major campaigns were described. Casualty statistics were not given, but, of course, the broadcasts created much worry and anxiety.

"We've heard a lot over the radio about the big air battles raging over there now. Every time I hear a broadcast like that, I think, 'I wonder if Art is in that one.' The suspense is something awful." – Ruth

With the mail in Buffalo interrupted by the storm, I'm sure my mother worried even more. But she found ways to cope.

"I've been looking over all of our pictures again. Sometimes, for a little while, I manage to recapture some of the happiness we had then. I almost relive every picture, trying to remember the things we said, the funny things that happened. Oh, wonderful photography! How it brings back the past." – Ruth

As the war went on, Art's family in Buffalo would sweat out the days worrying and trying to carry on with their lives. They were afraid every time the phone rang or someone pressed the door bell thinking they would hear the news that they dreaded most. Ruth wrote about one family's experience of just such a scenario.

"Walter Theisen's son was reported missing in action. Walter is an Iroquois Gas employee who rides in our car. The family had no word about the boy and naturally, they were very upset. The whole office took it to heart, too, and everyone felt almost as bad as Walter. Today, they received a letter from the son stating that he is a German prisoner and is safe and well. You should have seen that office when we heard the news! I had to go back into a corner and have a private little cry, and I have never even met the boy. But there were plenty of tear-filled eyes in the office. Walter was too stunned to cry. He just kept saying 'Thank God! Thank God!' and he shook like a leaf." – Ruth

Each letter from Art was a reassurance, tangible proof that he was still okay and a compounding hope that everything would be all right. Occasionally, newspaper articles offered added hope.

"Well, you old medal-wearer, you. Your name was in the paper tonight. Hmm, a celebrity! Congratulations Sergeant Haumesser! It's swell that you've gotten the Air Medal, but as far as I am concerned, I'd rather have you here next to me, undecorated, than to have you over there with millions of medals on you." – Ruth

In addition to radio, the American public scoured the newspapers for battle news during World War II. The U.S. military ran a strong public relations campaign to keep the folks back home upbeat and positive about the war efforts, sharing information with local papers about local boys. The article about my father and his brother Carl meeting in Europe is a perfect example.

My father's name would appear in the local Buffalo newspapers a few times for medals that he and the 463rd crew members were awarded. I don't ever remember him being boastful about his medals. In fact, they sat in a musty old metal box in his basement for years, hidden away until we found them when he had passed away.

Medals Awarded

DISTINGUISHED UNIT BADGE—Maj. Leo Hagerty and Staff Sgt. Russell E. Hansen, both in the China-Burma-India theater; Tech. Sgts. Joseph J. Gottstein and George M. Erikson, Staff Sgts. Thomas F. Clifford and Claybourne C. Thayer, Sgts. Arthur J. Haumesser, William E. Wannemacher and Richard Fernan, Corps. Roy W. Kintzel, John J. Ostapowicz, and Edward J. Kraft, and Pvt. Leon B. Kowalewski, all in Italy; Capt. Robert G. Burns, 2d Lt. Raymond A. Kennedy, Staff Sgt. Jerome Rosinski, Sgts. Albert J. Minotti, George W. Smith, and Stanley D. Cyranowski, all in France.

DISTINGUISHED UNIT BADGE AND ONE CLUSTER—2d Lt. Roy R. Roccon and Sgt. Charles Ciminesi, both in Italy.

COMBAT INFANTRYMAN'S BADGE—Pfc. Steven T. Pieri, Germany.

These men have been presented a blue battle ribbon at an Italian air base for "outstanding performance": Sgt. Thomas F. Clifford, 589 Linden Ave.; Sgt. Claybourne C. Thayer, 108 Oxford Ave.; Cpl. Roy W. Kintzel, 37 Knoerl Ave.; Pvt. Leon B. Kowalewski, 61 Rother Ave.; Cpl. John J. Ostapowicz, 61 Gibson St.; Sgt. William E. Wannemacher, 125 Folger St.; Sgt. Arthur J. Haumesser, 20 Columbus Ave.

Chapter 19 – Fighting the weather

"We're getting to be an awful lazy bunch of guys here. There's absolutely nothing to do all day long and when we could be doing something useful about the tent, what do we do but sit around and read." – Art

By January 1945, the weather in Italy had gone from bad to worse. Rain, snow and sleet had bombarded the Foggia area for weeks, turning the 463rd's base into a muddy bog that even the infamous Army jeeps could not navigate. The crews flew only four missions that month, as the runways and taxi strips turned into mucky streams. For the choir, trips up to see Padre Pio in San Giovanni were impossible as mountain roads were impassable.

"Still no letters written from my Arthur. What could it be? It must be the fault of the Post Office again. Of course it is. We won't discuss it any further. Blame it on the P.O." – Ruth

Just as a December snowstorm had idled mail delivery back in Buffalo, the nasty January weather forced a sudden slowdown of the mail delivery to and from Foggia. The idle time meant the men had more time to write letters, but the letters could not be delivered until weather improved.

My father and the crew flew on two of the four January missions. On the second mission of the new year, crews in the 774th targeted an oil refinery at Regensburg, Germany and a marshalling yard at Salzburg, Austria. My father's crew was part of Able company that split off to bomb the marshalling yard, destroying supply trains that delivered war goods to the Nazis. All the planes on that mission returned safely to Celone Field.

By this time, the Army Corp of Engineers had begun reinforcing and covering runways with pierced steel planking to combat the mud and muck. Several years ago, I spoke with a member of the 463rd who had returned to Foggia with his wife in the 1970s. He noted there was nothing left of anything he could recognize as Celone Field. However, some of the steel planking was still there, used by residents in Foggia as fencing or as walls for sheds and garages.

The 774th flew on another mission on the last day of January, part of 32 planes that took off for a large oil refinery at Moosbierbaum, Austria, about 25 miles northeast of Vienna near the Danube River. According to the 463rd yearbook, the day was clear and cold and the crews faced very little flak. Several planes ahead of the 774th were dropping propaganda leaflets for the Austrian people below. Crew members described the leaflets as sweeping past them like a raging snowstorm.

Mission by mission, the U.S. Army Air Corps was destroying Nazi Germany's ability to fight the war.

CHAPTER 20 – ROMAN HOLIDAY

Art far left in first row, with fellow soldiers on trip to Rome

"Now FOR SOME very important news! I am going to Rome! It was all arranged for six of us from the choir by Father Rice who arranged for the orders from our CO. I'll tell you about it soon and if you don't hear from me for a few days, don't worry. We leave Monday and are due back Saturday. I wish I could let Carl know but it's too late for that." – Art

In addition to trips to San Giovanni, Father Rice continued to look after his Catholic airmen, finagling a trip to Rome and the Vatican in early February when the weather began improving. A letter from my father to my mother about the trip suggests he was in his glory at the Vatican. Especially upon meeting Pope Pius XII.

"As I told you, we left here, eight of us, Father Rice and some of the choir, last Monday, one week ago, in a B-25. If it weren't for Father Rice, I would not be writing this now. No one was being sent to Rome rest camp for the past few weeks, but he saw Colonel McGregor, the CO, and had us put on orders for Rome. He also arranged for the B-25 Mitchell to take us there. Well, 45 minutes after taking off, we were in Rome.

"Tuesday morning, we headed for the Vatican where Father said mass in St. Peter's. It's so beautiful and immense it's hard to tell it in words. The first thing that strikes you is the size. St. Gerard's* could comfortably fit inside. But it is deceiving. The place is so perfectly proportional that things don't seem as large as they actually are.

"Then escorted by dignified looking men in tuxedos, we went past guards in brilliant uniforms and through rooms with bright red tapestries on the walls and with beautiful furniture. Finally, we arrived at the room where we would meet him.

Pope Pius XII handing out rosaries to soldiers, Art on far right

"The moment had arrived and His Holiness, resplendent in a white fur cape over white vestments, entered. Immediately we were at ease for just to see him relieved us. He spoke perfect English and asked about news from home, our mothers, families and sweethearts. Then he gave his blessing and he departed. Those ten minutes I shall never forget." – Art

Art's visit to Rome was certainly a privilege of being in the Army Air Corps in Italy. And it sure did impress my mother.

"Today I received that wonderful letter of yours in which you described your trip to Rome. I just can't tell you what a thrill it gives me to read that letter. To think that you have actually spoken to the Pope and received his blessing – well, it takes my breath away!

"Oh Art, I'm so glad you had the wonderful opportunity. I just can't get over it, that's all. I wandered around the house today saying to myself, 'My Arthur saw the Pope, he talked to him!'

"I let my family read the letter (all except the last page, that is). I hope you don't mind, Art. I wanted them to share in the wonder of it, too. Roy was put out because I wouldn't let him read the last paragraph of the letter." – Ruth

*St. Gerard's was Ruth's Catholic parish in Buffalo.

Chapter 21 – Wild blue yonder

"YOU SHOULD SEE us some of these mornings. Danny Harris, the operations clerk, comes around about 5:00 AM and opening the door and switching on the lights he says, 'Lieutenant Connor's crew, it's now 4:45 AM (it is actually 5:00 AM), be over at operations at 5:45.' Ten minutes later, someone says, 'Let's get up and eat.' There's a series of affirmative grunts and after another ten, we're dressed and on to the mess hall. You sweat out a line for five minutes, eat and then, of course, must have a smoke over that cup of coffee and discuss where we might be going that day. It's now about 5:35 AM.

"Back to the tent and a last check to see that you have plenty of cigarettes, candy and other stuff. Oh yes, and now we have to feed the dog. It's now about 5:50, so off we go to operations just about in time to catch a truck down to the briefing. That is, pilot, navigator, bombardier and myself go to the briefing.

"The other boys get our stuff (flying equipment) from the building where they keep it for us and go out to the ship assigned to us. Briefing is over soon and then we go out to the ship and usually culminate a busy morning by waiting an hour or hour and a half waiting for take-off time. Of course, we have to install our guns and check equipment on the ship but that doesn't take long. It doesn't sound like a very trying beginning for the day, but it becomes pretty hectic at times.

"I'm feeling pretty tired right now, having flown a mission today. It feels as though we'd done eight hours of rock-breaking at the end of the day. You usually have a splitting headache, too, to make things even more cheerful. It's caused by breathing that oxygen for so long." – Art

The war went on and the letters kept crossing the sea, back and forth. Missions left the crew numb with fatigue and the mental strain of trying to stay alive through flak, artillery fire, enemy fighters and German rockets. My father used to say he was glad he wasn't on the ground with the infantry, but would point out that there were no foxholes in which to hide on a B-17. No retreating into the woods. The sky could become a graveyard in an instant, as wounded planes fell like sheet metal coffins to total destruction on the earth below.

Men faced these trials by cementing bonds with their fellow airmen that went far beyond a typical friendship. They were packed in it together, not only on missions, but in the waiting hours between, in the lonely village of tents that made up the base. The choir certainly strengthened those bonds, especially between my father and crew member, Ernie Conrad, the flight engineer. Their bond had already become unbreakable when Art helped save Ernie's life.

Added danger

As if facing German fighters wasn't bad enough, B-17 crews had to worry about anoxia. Anoxia – a lack of oxygen – was a constant threat that could kill in an instant.

The oxygen system on the B-17 required each crew member to wear an oxygen mask with a main hose connected to the front. They would begin using oxygen at 10,000 feet and above, and the system mixed outside air with pure oxygen. Too much pure oxygen caused the splitting headache my dad described in his letter. Lack of oxygen could be deadly in just a few seconds. A navigator from the 772nd squadron had died of anoxia on the same day that my father flew his first mission with the 463rd.

My father didn't brag about helping to save Ernie's life, but rather was humble when speaking of it. He described the incident in a letter to a fellow veteran in later years.

"All of us knew the danger of lack of oxygen. We were trained in how to be aware of it and of how sinister its effects on a crewman were. I no longer remember the mission, the date, the target but I will always recall it. We were at altitude, well into the mission. In the layout of the B-17, when the bomb bay cabin doors were open, it was possible for the radio operator to look directly forward into the cockpit area including the upper gun turret and the flight engineer's position.

"The first time I looked forward I noticed that Ernie was down on the floor. This was not unusual since the fuel tank valves were located in that same area so I turned back to my desk and resumed my job at the radio.

"Five or ten seconds later for some reason I know not why I looked through that opening once more. Ernie appeared to me in exactly the same position as before. He had not moved one bit. A call to co-pilot Bill Deane alerted him to the situation and he discovered that Ernie's oxygen hose had somehow become disconnected from the mask and that he was unconscious.

"Happily, Ernie recovered consciousness but it could have been fatal in a matter of seconds. To this day I will never understand why I took a second look but I like to think that Ernie's guardian angel wanted me to help since he and I were such good friends." – Art

Purple Heart kid

On February 22, planes from the 15th Air Force joined planes from the 8th, 9th and 12th Air Forces to bomb communications targets throughout Germany and Austria. My father's crew was in one of twenty-five B-17s that dropped 73 tons of bombs that day.

On the crew's return to home base, they encountered heavy flak over Northern Italy, in an area still held by the Germans. Right waist gunner Robert Burns was hit.

"I've been keeping something from you about Bob. Perhaps I should have told you when it happened but I wasn't sure whether I should. On a mission over Northern Italy, he was hit in the leg by a piece of flak. It wasn't very serious; a piece about as big as your little fingernail hit him just above the knee and put him in the hospital for a few weeks. He's okay now, so we have a Purple Heart kid with us." – Art

What my father didn't tell my mother in the letter was that he was the one who tended to the injured gunner and administered morphine to Burns. The wound was bigger than a "fingernail" as my father described in his letter so as not to worry my mother.

My father, up toward the front of the plane away from Burns, radioed the pilot and co-pilot that the waist gunner was hit. The flak or shrapnel tore through the leather flight suit and gashed Burns' leg. Grabbing the on-board medical kit, Art and the other crew members helped put on a tourniquet to stop the bleeding. Coming in to land at the base, the B-17 crew fired off two flares to indicate wounded on board. Burns spent almost three weeks in an Army hospital in Italy before returning to fly with the crew.

It was considered good luck if a crew member was hit by a piece of flak without serious injuries, so Burns became their good luck charm as the missions continued.

My father said he was once hit by a piece of flak – it felt like a tap on his shoulder and didn't rip into the flight suit he recalled – and he kept it in his tent, on the nightstand. He said the piece disappeared one day and he always thought that a fellow airman had swiped it for good luck. Such was the superstition regarding flak.

Ruth with Pudgie, the family dog

"Enclosed please find one gray hair pulled from my head today. Reason for one gray hair? Two years of worrying about a certain GI I call Arthur Joseph Haumesser." – Ruth

While my mother wasn't meeting popes and future saints like her fiancé, Ruth was swept up in the war efforts back home. She was on an entertainment committee for the USO chapter in Buffalo. She was a donor at Red Cross blood drives. She worked her office job at the Iroquois Gas Company. She also took a part time job in the evenings sorting mail at the post office downtown. And she worried.

But the letters – tailwinds for her as well as my father – helped her through.

"I've found a sure fire way to dream of you – it works every time. At night, just before I turn out the light, I read a few of your letters, and a few minutes later, sure enough, I meet you in dream land. Such nice dreams I have, too. I can never remember details in the dawn's early light, but just the thought that we were together for a little while warms me through and through." – Ruth

Her letters also continued to keep my father up to date on things back home, including how his widowed and war weary mother was doing.

"Your mother told me that Virginia and Ray sold their house and are going to move in with her. That's good news, I think. It'll be good for your mother to have a man in the house until you boys get back. And the kids will help to keep her mind off other things, too." – Ruth

My Aunt Virginia and Uncle Ray Petty moved in with my grandmother on Columbus Avenue for a short time, through the end of the war and the following couple of years. They eventually moved to a house in the suburbs of Buffalo and my grandmother continued to live with them until she passed in the 1970s.

In addition to letters, Ruth would send Art packages with film, books, hair tonic, cookies and other niceties he could not obtain in Italy.

"Every time I see something to put in a box for you, I buy it and stick it in my dresser drawer until I get a request letter. Well, I saw a small box of cheese tidbits one day and I brought them home and stuck them in my bottom drawer.

"The other night I opened the drawer to get something and left it open a little. I was in the kitchen and suddenly Pudgie came tearing out of my bedroom with something in his mouth. What was it but that box of cheese tidbits! That cur!

"He nicely took off the outside wrapper, chewed through the cardboard box and then proceeded to eat the crackers. I was so mad, I could have throttled him, but it struck me as being funny after a while and I had a good laugh." – Ruth

Support for the war effort in Buffalo continued and my mother also kept Art posted on various happenings in the city.

"Bob Hope was in Buffalo today. They had a parade down Main Street and he and Jerry Colonna* were riding in an open jeep waving to everyone. I saw them from from the office window. A few of the girls went down and were standing right next to him. They were so excited, they couldn't work for the rest of the afternoon." – Ruth

And like Art, Ruth kept the faith.

"I went over to St. Michael's Church after shopping downtown today. It's odd, but when I'm in that church, I feel so close to you. Perhaps it's because I know you were in there quite often when you attended Canisius." – Ruth

Jerry Colonna was a popular sidekick of Bob Hope in his films in the 1940s and 1950s.

Chapter 23 – Dog days

"We have yet another occupant in our tent. In fact, we only acquired it tonight. Well, I gave it away with 'it' but I couldn't very well say 'her' for it's a female puppy that now enjoys our company. I don't know what kind it is but we are hoping it won't turn out to be a Great Dane or St. Bernard. It was running loose around the chapel and even came in during mass so Ernie sort of adopted her." – Art

In addition to the choir and visits to Padre Pio, another comfort for my father and his crew mates was a puppy they cleverly named Veni Qua – "come here" in Italian. They fed her from scraps and such from the mess hall and let her sleep the day away in their tent.

Veni became a sort of mascot for the 774th squadron and she certainly would have had a calming effect on the soldiers, especially when they returned from a mission. In a later letter, toward the end of the war, my father wrote that Veni Qua had run away and they had not seen her for weeks. Given the poverty and scarcity of food around Foggia, my dad often wondered if the dog was taken by a villager for purposes other than a friendly pet.

CHAPTER 24 - AMERICAN PRIDE

"Yesterday, I experienced a genuine thrill. We were coming home over the Adriatic after a successful mission. I was tuned in on the American Expeditionary station in Foggia and they were playing some fine military music. I happened to glance out of my window and the sight of these planes filling the sky made me feel very proud. Some of these guys might call me crazy for saying this, but I don't know how anyone could look at these silver ships against the blue of the sea and the sky and not have just a little feeling of pride. It clears up a lot of things. I thank God that I'm privileged to fly with them and not be against them." – Art

A mission on February 25 was another rugged one for the 463rd. On the way to the target, as they approached Munich, they met a heavy barrage of flak and rockets. At Linz, the target, the planes made another run through heavy flak, dropping 77 tons of bombs. Two crews were lost to the intense flak barrage.

On the return home, most certainly pumped up on adrenaline, my father noted the inspiring site he described above, in a letter to my mother. But he never mentioned the lost crews. In most of his letters, he tried to stay upbeat and positive for my mother's sake, sharing what details he could without being censored. He filled her in with with trivial facts about air corps life.

"No crew has what may be called their own ship so we don't have a name for our B-17. The battle order is put up the night before we fly with the number of the ship we are to fly and that is the one we fly." - Art

While Hollywood movies such as "The Memphis Belle" would lead you to believe each crew had their own plane, in reality, as my dad pointed out, it was rare if ever true, especially toward the end of the war. Planes were damaged during missions. They required constant maintenance. So it simply isn't logical that a crew had the same plane every mission. Each plane of the 463rd did have a distinct tail marking – the letter Y on an inverted, arced triangle, with a yellow rudder.

Nonetheless, B-17 bombers were mass produced and no two planes flew alike. They had their own personalities which led the crews to christen them with a name and decorate them with nose art. Some of the names given to the Flying Fortresses of the 463rd by the crews included:

The Bellringer	Flying Beast	Dottie Bee
Hell n Back	The Atoner	Miss Peggy
Flak Happy	Hell On Wings	Old Ironsides
Raidin' Maiden	Homesick Angel	Bigass Bird

Try as he might to spare my mother the terrifying details of the air war, his survival of one particularly brutal mission caused Art to write with more information than ever.

CHAPTER 25 – TARGET BERLIN

"BY THE TIME you receive this letter you probably will have heard of the mission we flew yesterday. It should get a lot of attention because it was never done before and we set a new record. Yesterday, honey, we bombed Berlin. That may not seem novel or strange to you for you read of Berlin being bombed every day. But for us here in Italy to fly all the way up there is news. It was an awfully long trip, too long in fact because we didn't get all the way back here. I don't usually tell you all the details of the missions because I know you'll worry, but everything turned out all right for us on this one, so I'll tell you.

"About half an hour before we reached the target, we ran into some very heavy flak, the worst I have ever seen. It put number three engine out of commission but we continued on to Berlin, dropped our eggs and turned for home. After about half of the way home, we realized we'd never be able to reach the base on what gas we had left despite the fact that we threw out a lot of stuff.

"There was no need to worry, though, for within easy range was an emergency field in Yugoslavia. So that's where we headed and finally landed. One hour later, we were in another ship heading home. They say we made history yesterday, but I'm not anxious to do it again. That's another reason I mentioned it, because we didn't do it without a cost." – Art

The 463rd Bomb Group led an historic mission to bomb Berlin. My father's plane is 700 in Dog company. Six planes shaded indicate crews lost on the mission, representing 60 men lost.

THE ROUGHEST MISSION

BY FEBRUARY 1945, THERE was a resurgence of German air strength around Berlin to protect the capital. The 463rd would meet this fighting power head on during a mission to Berlin that became historic for the number of planes flown and for how deep they were able to fly into Germany.

As my dad noted in his letter, the mission was unique. The Nazis expected Allied bombing raids that deep to come from Great Britain to the west, not Italy to the south. The 15th Air Force bombers had never flown so far before on a mission – 9 hours 10 minutes versus an average 7.5 hours. On the trip they would encounter batteries of huge antiaircraft guns and the best German fighters left in the Nazi air force.

My brother and I joined my parents for a 463rd Bomb Group reunion in Arizona in 2002. I had interviewed a number of the veterans at the reunion for an article I was writing for the local newspaper in Buffalo. When I asked about the Berlin mission, responses were either silence, as though they did not wish to talk about it, or rage that it was an unnecessary mission that some higher up created for an extra medal or something. Either way, it was obvious the Berlin mission was terrifying and affected them profoundly.

One veteran described the ship's four, 12-cylinder engines roaring as they clawed through the air on takeoff. Those engines could put out 1,350 horsepower, but the bomb loads were heavy and on the Berlin mission, the ships lumbered through the air. The creaking of the plane and cry of the whooshing wind would keep time with the nervous breathing of the soldiers on the long journey. They might talk on the interphone, telling jokes, singing, anything to take their minds off what waited ahead.

Crews were very experienced by this point – in fact Berlin was my father's 20th mission. And the 463rd had already earned a Distinguished Unit Citation for bombing oil refineries in Ploesti, Romania in May of 1944. But this was different.

CATCHING FLAK

THE 463RD BOMB GROUP was in the lead and the formation of B-17s was met by heavy flak as soon as they crossed the Alps. Exhilaration would have swept over the crew, as their ships were rocked by blasts of heavy metal shrapnel.

The encounter threw many planes off course, but pushing ahead they reconnected and flew on to the target. I'm guessing this is where the third engine of my father's plane – as described in his letter – would have been damaged.

Once they neared Berlin, the bombers were met by more heavy flak as well as German fighter planes attacking from the north. More exhilaration. The bombers were escorted and protected by P-51 and P-38 fighter planes.

But the gunners on the B-17s would be in the fight, firing at attacking enemy planes as the Fortresses shuddered. Shouts over the interphone. Floating wisps of smoke from the blazing guns. Empty shell casings scattered from the 50 millimeters.

HEAVY LOSSES

AS MY FATHER said in his letter, they didn't complete the mission without cost. Six planes – 60 airmen – were lost from the 774th alone. Twelve other planes – 120 airmen – were lost from other groups of the 15th Air Force on the Berlin mission. The 463rd dropped 50 tons of bombs on Daimler-Benz tank factories and assembly plants that were crucial to the Nazi's continued fight in the war.

As my father also wrote, their number three engine was shot out. To lighten the load, the crew tossed out heavy items not critical to the return trip of the plane such as the bomb racks. A popular song during the war – *"Comin' in on a Wing and a Prayer"* – about a damaged plane returning to base could have been written about the crew on the Berlin mission:

Comin' in on a wing and a prayer
Comin' in on a wing and a prayer
With our one motor gone
We can still carry on
Comin' in on a wing and a prayer

What a show, what a fight
Boys, we really hit our target for tonight
How we sing as we limp through the air
Look below, there's our field over there
With our one motor gone
We can still carry on
Comin' in on a wing and a prayer

I only learned about the emergency landing in Yugoslavia from my father's letter. He never spoke about it. I imagine that's because the mission was one of his most traumatic experiences during the war, as it was for so many of the elderly veterans I met at the 463rd reunion in Arizona.

Post traumatic stress disorder – PTSD – was not a recognized diagnosis after World War II. Battle scarred vets were said to have shell shock, manifested in extreme cases as psychological disorders and alcohol abuse, and in lesser cases as stoic silence. My father chose the latter. By his own admission, Art's faith was the biggest reason he was able to keep it together and his Padre Pio experiences played a part.

Ruth's own strong faith helped even more. Here is how she responded after learning about the Berlin mission.

"I just read the letter in which you told me about your mission over Berlin. I've looked up the distance on a map and I wouldn't believe it possible if you hadn't told me about it. Thank God things turned out all right for you on that mission. You say you made that mission on March 24. That was the day we received our rosaries and used them for the first time, too. Of course, we're praying constantly but I'll bet those prayers on those rosaries blessed by the Pope had a lot to do with your safety on that mission. You know, after this war, I'm going to spend the rest of my life saying thank you to the dear Lord for bringing you home safely to me." – Ruth

CHAPTER 26 - BATTLE HONORS

THE 463RD RECEIVED ITS second Distinguished Unit Citation (DUC) for the Berlin mission for damaging tank factories at the Daimler-Benz assembly plant. The 463rd yearbook described the mission.

"Carrying a load of 1,000 pounders, the 463rd led the Fifth Wing on a record-breaking flight to the Daimler-Benz tank works in Berlin on the 24th. Six ships were lost en route to the target. At Berlin, the formation was jumped by a large number of jet-propelled German 262s. Group gunners claimed one definite and several probables."

The Citation follows, as written by the War Department, offering great detail on what the planes encountered.

Distinguished Unit Citation - Presented by the War Department

The 463rd Bombardment Group is cited for outstanding performance of duty in armed conflict with the enemy. On 24 March 1945, this group was notified to prepare maximum aircraft to lead a wing formation on a mission to attack and destroy the Daimler-Benz Tank Works in Berlin, Germany.

A successful completion of this mission would materially reduce the enemy hopes of a prolonged defensive against the Red Army then deployed on the eastern bank of the Oder River. Realizing the strategic importance of this undertaking, the deepest escorted penetration ever attempted in the European Theater of Operations, and one hitherto deemed all but impossible from bases in Southern Italy, the ground crews enthusiastically and sedulously labored day and night to bring all available aircraft to the peak of mechanical efficiency despite the extensive battle damages incurred in the almost daily operations of the preceding month.

Operations and Intelligence personnel indefatigably applied their greatest efforts to supply the carefully selected crews with vital bombing and target data. On 24 March 1945, thirty-one B-17 type aircraft loaded with maximum bombing tonnage took off, made rendezvous with other groups of the wing, and after assuming the lead, set course for the objective.

The Alps crossed, and having bypassed all known flak areas in Austria and Czechoslovakia, the group had almost entered Germany proper when suddenly and without warning it was savagely opposed by a concentrated and sustained antiaircraft barrage which inflicted heavy damage to the nearly entire formation and destroyed four heavy bombers. Despite the intensity and accuracy of the heavy guns, the gallant crews battled their way through the enemy defenses, reformed the temporarily demoralized and scattered aircraft of the wing, and were successful in holding the entire formation intact at this critical stage of the flight.

Passing out of the effective range of the gun emplacements, the battered group was immediately attacked by 15 jet-propelled enemy fighters firing cannon and rockets, which were only dispersed by the belated but aggressive appearance of friendly fighters after another bomber was destroyed in the running battle.

As the flight continued, the crippled airplanes were realigned into three squadrons for the dual purpose of protective cover and bombing accuracy. Nearing the specific target, the flak-riddled formation was for the third time subjected to a stiffened enemy resistance with a sixth ship shot down, but not withstanding the severe damage sustained by the aircraft, the unnerving experiences just passed, the improvised character of the formation, the last minute changes of bombing calculations, and the weariness induced by many hours spent at high altitude, the 463rd Bombardment Group relentlessly and unswervingly led the entire wing formation through for an exceptionally successful bombing run, with the complete bomb tonnage of its formation concentrated in the target area, thus inflicting extensive damage to vital enemy installations and supplies so greatly needed by the enemy in its defense of the capital city. Turning off the target, the doughty but damaged formation rallied and turned for home.

The long and still hazardous trip through heavily defended enemy terrain over mountainous regions and finally over water was too great a strain for 6 of the 20 airplanes which had reached the heart of the enemy's productive system, and these were forced down at friendly fields in Northern Italy and Yugoslavia for medical treatment to the many wounded men as well as mechanical repairs to the crippled aircraft.

Only 14 of the original attacking force were successful in reaching their home base, but in no instance was there a reported case of insufficient gas supply, so brilliantly had this mission been planned and so skillfully flown. By the conspicuous courage, airmanship, and determination of the combat crews, together with the outstanding professional skill and devotion to duty of the maintenance crews, the 463rd Bombardment Group upheld the highest traditions of the military service, thereby reflecting great credit on itself and the armed forces of the United States.

– General Orders 3338 Headquarters Fifteenth Air Force 3 July 1945 as approved by the Commanding General, Mediterranean Theater –

CHAPTER 27 – COUNTING DOWN

"I'M FEELING PRETTY happy tonight. Cause for the main and simple reason I have been flying, flying, and flying. I put in four this week which leaves me nine to go." – Art

In mid-April, the choir returned to visit Padre Pio, the first time in two months since they had seen him. Father Rice treated the members to dinner at the inn, and while he and another soldier had to return to base, my father and the rest of the choir spent the night.

Later on, back at the base, the camp was buzzing with the news – President Franklin Roosevelt had died. My father wrote home:

"So now we have a new president, or, rather in my case, a new commander-in-chief. I heard it first in the chow line this morning and didn't quite believe it, but it's true. Roosevelt was a good man and a fine president. It will take a very capable man to fill his place." – Art

As he counted down the missions in the letters to my mother, Art gave some more insight into some of those missions.

"I flew my first mission as a panther* operator today. I was having lots of fun chasing "Fritz" around the frequencies. I'd pick up his radar signal at a certain frequency and then jam it. Then a little later, I'd find that he'd moved his frequency up a little. So I'd move right up on top of him. He'd move. I'd move. I could just see him pulling out his hair and pounding his head in his little Wurzburg." – Art

And he counted.

"I flew with a crew whose pilot finished up today. It's quite an occasion when one of the officers finishes. First of all, there's a grand display of flares as you circle the field for a landing. When we rolled to a stop, there was one of his buddies to meet him with a brand new bottle of Schenley's. Everyone has a drink including the ground crew. Didn't take long for that quart to go dry with all those guys around. Boy, how I wish I was in their shoes; but some day very soon, I will be." – Art

Meanwhile, Ruth waited.

"Maybe these months will fly by. Oh, I hope so, because the days are just dragging, endlessly, for me, too. Never mind, some day all this waiting will be just a memory, something to look back upon and then be glad it's all over." – Ruth.

Panther was a new radio system used by the U.S. Army Air Corps toward the end of the war

CHAPTER 28 – RETURN TO ROTONDO

In San Giovanni, Art on left in second last row, Father Rice on right behind children

"WE ARE ALWAYS accompanied by at least four Italian kids. Some of them speak a little English but all that most of them know is, 'Hey, candy Joe!' You'd meet them everywhere you went." - Art

I can gather from the letters that the choir and my father visited Padre Pio a couple of more times as spring weather improved travel.

"I am going up to San Giovanni tomorrow morning with Father Rice and the choir. Padre Pio's niece is getting married – or someone related to him anyway – and we've been invited. I'll tell you all about it soon." – Art

"We returned to the monastery around twelve. They were giving a dinner for the children and this time we helped out. It's a wonder we got out alive. We had brought with us a lot of extra candy and this and a lot of other stuff that other fellows brought before us was dumped into baskets. Then began the massacre. It started out very orderly by going along each table but these kids hadn't seen candy in months it seemed and you know how they like candy.

"Well, pretty soon all there was, was one milling throng of yelling, screaming and some crying ones. Whew! What a gang, but it was fun." – Art

The last letter that mentions a visit to Padre Pio was dated mid April and it appears that was the final visit to San Giovanni. My father and his crew flew nine missions in April which would have left little time off to travel up the mountain to see the priest.

Soon, there was good news that turned my father's attention to coming home.

CHAPTER 29 – FAREWELL TO ARMS

"Darling, now that my combat days are over, I want to thank you from the bottom of my heart for the love, for the devotion, you've shown during these long months. Without it, I don't know what I would have done. I was determined to come through all right because I knew what I would have to come home to. More than that, though, I want to thank you especially for your prayers on my behalf. That they helped, and helped immensely, there is no doubt. Not only did you persuade God to spare me but knowing that you were there praying for me, made me feel so much more at ease in the face of danger. When I get home you shall be repaid a thousand fold with all the love and esteem I can muster. Good night, darling. I love you so much." – Art

Being engaged to my mother was another of Art's powerful tailwinds – the determination to return home safely to her love. April 26, 1945 was the 222nd, and final, combat mission flown by the 463ʳᵈ Bomb Group.

By May of 1945, my father had flown 30 missions over German targets – over 213 hours in the air. When Germany signed an unconditional surrender on May 7, the the 463ʳᵈ airmen were no longer a combat unit.

774TH MISSION HISTORY

Number	Date	Sorties	Target	Time
1	11/11/41	1	Salzburg, Austria	7:30
2	11/16/44	2	Innsbruck, Austria	7:50
3	11/17/44	7	Salzburg, Austria	8:40
4	11/18/44	4	Vienna, Austria	7:40
5	11/19/44	6	Vienna, Austria	7:30

6	12/9/44	9	Regensburg, Germany	8:05
7	1/20/44	10	Salzburg, Austria	8:15
8	1/31/45	12	Moosbierbaum, Austria	7:50
9	2/1/45	13	Graz, Austria	6:50
10	2/14/45	15	Vienna, Austria	6:45
11	2/16/44	16	Bolzano, Italy	7:30
12	2/18/45	18	Vienna, Austria	7:30
13	2/22/44	19	Salzburg, Austria	8:15
14	2/25/45	21	Linz, Austria	7:25
15	2/28/45	22	Verona, Italy	5:55
16	3/2/45	24	Linz, Austria	6:50
17	3/16/45	26	Schwechat, Austria	6:20
18	3/20/45	28	Kagran, Austria	7:10
19	3/22/45	30	Ruhland, Germany	8:40
20	3/24/45	32	Berlin, Germany	9:10
21	4/1/45	33	Maribor Bridge, Yugoslavia	5:40
22	4/5/45	34	Udine, Italy	6:00
23	4/7/45	34	Verona, Italy	7:30
24	4/15/45	35	Buckland Operations, Area M-23	6:30
25	4/16/45	36	Buckland Operations, Area M-23	5:30
26	4/17/45	37	Buckland Operations, Area MA-23	5:35
27	4/20/45	38	Fortezza, Italy	6:55
28	4/23/45	39	Bonavigo, Italy	6:00
29	4/24/45	40	Malborghetto, Italy	6:15
30	4/26/45	42	Bronzolo, Italy	6:10

Total Time: 213:45

*774th Mission History Certified Correct – Oren K. Crum, Major, Air Corps Operations Officer

Final numbers for the group's operations according to the 463rd yearbook were:

- Total Sorties – 6,966
- Combat Hours – 45,764
- Bomb Tonnage Dropped – 16,868
- Enemy Planes Destroyed – 80
- 463rd Planes Lost in Combat – 106
- 463rd Soldiers Lost – 1,065

Chapter 30 – Homebound Task Force

"I FLEW IN one of the converted B-17s yesterday and believe me it was a nostalgic experience. I could almost get poetic about it. I mean the tame and un-ferocious appearance of it. Everything warlike being removed. The waist has a broad floor and benches in it as does my radio room. You can actually walk through without banging your head a few times. The radio equipment has been put in the nose where I shall fly from now on. The bomb bay that used to carry so much destruction now has baggage racks. Oh well, it should make me feel glad for it's sort of a symbol that this war is over." - Art

The 463rd became part of the military's Homebound Task Force created to take on the monumental task of returning American soldier's home from the European front after Germany's surrender. Joining forces with the 383rd Bomb Group, the former bomber crews would be transporting troops from the Fifth Army, flying from Naples, Italy to Casablanca, Morocco, a 1,380 mile trip that took about seven and a half hours.

Ground crews removed the planes' armor plating, oxygen systems, machine guns, bomb racks, turrets and any weight not essential to this new assignment. Seats were installed to carry from 15 to 20 passengers in the waist and radio sections.

His new assignment meant Art would not be coming home any time soon. But as my mother expressed in a letter, transporting troops was much better than the alternative.

"Of course, I am unhappy because you're not coming home as soon as we expected, but as the days roll by, I can see more and more that it's for the best. Why, only the other night, there was a picture in the paper of a ship landing in New York which carried members of the 15th Air Force. The caption said they were on their way to the Pacific via the U.S. The thought that you might have been one of them soon to go to the Pacific makes me shudder. It's hard, this waiting, but if it means your safety and well-being, I think we can both stand it for a while longer." – Ruth

By the end of June, the 463rd had carried nearly 5,000 veteran troops to Morocco. Through July and August, my father and other crews operated steadily, transporting what amounted to several Army divisions – more than 20,000 GIs – over many, many flights.

"We returned from another trip to Africa today. This trip was a first in my flying career. For the first time, I flew with women aboard. Yes, we carried a load of 19 WACs* and one nurse this time." – Art

Back at the air base in Celone, tents were taken down, lumber and scrap metal was piled up, and surplus and salvageable equipment was neatly stacked. The bomb group retained only a small number of soldiers at the base. Most of the officers and enlisted men left for the States, were transferred to various units around Europe, or were awaiting shipment home. My father was eventually stationed in Naples.

*Women's Army Corps

"FATHER RICE DROPPED into the tent this morning to say good-bye. He's moving today, and since we are going to Naples soon, we probably won't see him again. He said he would stop in Buffalo some time if he got the chance." – Art

As the war with Germany came to an end, officers and GIs were transferred to other posts or sent home. Father George Rice was reassigned to another group in Northern Italy and left the 463rd in June.

The man who had watched out for young Art when the soldier learned that his dad had passed – a surrogate father for the airman in a way – was soon gone. My father had to feel the loss, as he in particular among the choir members had grown very close to the chaplain.

Art had volunteered to help Father Rice in his office, filing, typing let-

95

ters, addressing letters and so on. In return, Captain Rice recommended Art for an Enlisted Man Commendation which he received from Lt. Col. Charles F. Scott, Commanding Officer in the Army Air Corps. My dad was as proud of that commendation as he was of any of the medals he was awarded during the war. And Art had held a special place in the chaplain's heart.

"Today I received a pleasant surprise – a letter from your chaplain, Father Rice. I think it's a wonderful gesture of Father's to go to the trouble of sending letters to we folks at home. I felt very humbled indeed when I read one sentence in the letter – he looks to Jesus, Mary and you for inspiration. To be put in the same category with Jesus and Mary is certainly something to make one humble. I'll try not to gripe so much in the future. Every time I feel myself getting in a mood, I'll read Father's letter again, and he will set me straight." – Ruth

Father Rice wrote to my dad upon returning to the U.S. explaining where the priest ended up after leaving the 463rd.

"After three weeks in Pisa we broke up and all came back to Foggia and the 99th Bomb Group. Then over to Camp Marcianise (near Caserta) where they deactivated two outfits under us and left some of us high and dry. But there was lots of spare time, a jeep and Rome not so far away. Then I was assigned to the Service Group in Naples. Nice chapel, office, living quarters and a German POW (good man) to take care of everything. We had midnight mass last Christmas in the post theater with about 400 Germans present and singing Stille Nacht. I avoided shipment until after the cardinals' consistory in Rome in February. I then sailed on a victory ship in March and arrived at Camp Kilmer (in New Jersey) on March 28." – Father George Rice

In addition to Father Rice, several crew members had already gone home and the ranks of the 774th squadron continued to slowly thin. Without Father Rice, the choir was disbanded and the trips to see Padre Pio would not happen without the chaplain's leadership.

My father never mentioned going to see Padre Pio on his own, and the end of the visits must have seemed abrupt. Art probably imagined returning to San Giovanni some day, as a civilian, but it never happened. Yet, Padre Pio's influence never stopped and my father would no doubt think of him often through the war's end.

CHAPTER 32 – EYE ON JAPAN

"I RECEIVED THE wonderful news of Japan's possible surrender while with Carl yesterday. It sounds too good to be true. I've been taking a pessimistic view, planning to be in the Army at least another year. Now, if Japan surrenders, it means I may even be a civilian by next spring. I don't think we should leave the emperor to go free as they want. His influence with the masses is too great to be allowed to continue, to be used again in the future to arouse the people to war.

"It won't take much longer anyhow. That atomic bomb is a terrible weapon to use, even against the Japanese, and it should make them surrender, emperor or not." - Art

News of Japan's surrender was announced on August 15, 1945. A big, collective sigh of relief must have been heard from the remaining men of the 463rd. Finally, they knew for sure that they would not be sent to fight in the Pacific Theater.

"Are you feeling pretty happy tonight? I know I am for at long last our prayers have been answered. It's too wonderful to believe, no more war, the world is at peace again, after so long.

"Know where I heard the news first? I was sound asleep in the airplane at Port Lyautey (one of the newer unpleasant duties is that someone must stay with the ship all night) when about 5 AM I was awakened by a screaming siren. Looking out, I saw flares going off so I knew what it must mean. I turned on the radio and got the wonderful news. I went to eat and after we took off I picked up a broadcast from the states. They were broadcasting the celebrations in Times Square, New York and all the major U.S. cities. It sure sounded great!" – Art

Back home, spontaneous VJ Day celebrations had erupted throughout downtown Buffalo. Military leaders signed the official surrender of Japan on the USS Missouri on September 2, 1945. War was over.

"I've been thinking of you twice as much lately. Thinking of all the wonderful times we have had, and dreaming of the wonderful times we are going to have. I've been thinking about what I am going to say when I first see you. No, I don't think I'll say anything at all – actions speak louder than words, don't they? Oooh, I get all shivery when I think about that wonderful day! Oh, dear God, please make it soon…very soon." – Ruth

Chapter 33 – When in Naples

Art during some R&R on the Isle of Capri, 1945

"It's a beautiful morning here in Naples and as I look out across the bay of Naples from the patio of this pleasant villa, I can see the white-sailed fishing boats and in the distance the faint outline of Capri." – Art

As my father continued to transport troops into September, he and his friend Ernie Conrad were stationed in an apartment in Naples. At one point, one of the commanding officers asked the two if they would like a good deal, instead of the usual work detail to which they would be assigned when not flying – KP duty in the mess halls, airplane tasks, etc.

The two airmen accepted when they heard it meant living in the Air Corps officer's club in Naples. Formerly a yacht club, the building was now being used by officers who were coming and going on their way back to the states.

Ernie and my father worked nights at the club "selling membership cards and bar books" according to one of my father's letters.

"The sad part is that we didn't get this deal a while ago for we'll be here only a few days. They are moving the crews out very fast back at the base. We'll be transferred to the 515th in maybe a week for final processing and then it's homeward bound.

"Soon, my darling, very soon, I'll be flying straight homes to the arms of the one person in this world I love with all my heart. I'll Be Seeing You."
– Art

The distance from Naples to San Giovanni Rotondo was likely the biggest factor in my father and Ernie not returning to visit Padre Pio. New duties transporting troops kept them busy and furloughs were no longer offered, as men were finally heading home for good.

Not that my father would ever forget Padre Pio, but now the soldier's focus was on getting back home to Buffalo.

CHAPTER 34 – THE HOMECOMING

"WE MAY BE here a bit longer than four or five days. It seems someone over at Pomigliano was off the ball. There are 127 engines to be changed on the ships over there. Any engines with over a certain number of hours on them have to be changed for new ones before making the crossing. With luck, we may leave in a week. The colonel said that we would most likely fly home as passengers and that we'd be out of Italy by the end of the month. He also assured us that we are going home – that is a definite." – Art

In September of 1945, an order from the 15th Air Force officially deactivated the 463rd Bomb Group. My father and the remaining airmen of the Fighting 463rd were finally headed home. But the anticipation would continue to build, with delay after delay, and rumored plans suddenly changing at the last minute. Ruth's patience was tested.

"Last night at the show, I saw couples all around us, holding hands and sitting close together. I could have cried. When I see a love scene in a movie, I try to put you and me in the hero and heroine's places but it just doesn't seem to work. Nothing will do but the real thing. Our only consolation is prayer, a prayer that this awful war will be over very soon, and you and I, and couples all over the world will be able to continue our romance personally, not by proxy via the movies or by pen and ink." – Ruth

There was talk my father and fellow airmen would take a troop ship home from Morocco where they had been transporting ground troops. Then they learned at a briefing they would likely get to fly home, only this time as passengers not crew members.

"I'm going to make this a short one because I haven't much to tell you but what I do have is enough.

"Tonight will be my last night on Italian soil. Yes, tomorrow morning we take off for Marrakesh, Africa on the first leg of our journey home. I don't know what the route will be from there on. For the last time from overseas, here's all my love." – Art

From Naples, my father flew to Marrakesh and left there on September 23 on a flight to Dakar, Africa. From there he hopscotched toward home stopping in Brazil, British Guiana, Puerto Rico and finally Morrison Field in Florida. After 36 hours of flying time over six days, my father was on U.S. soil on September 29. Some troop ships crossing the Atlantic may have gotten him home a day or two earlier, but my dad was glad not to have been packed onto a crowded Victory ship carrying as many as 5,000 men.

After processing at Morrison Field, Art would take a train from Florida to Buffalo and be home the first week of October 1945. There don't seem to be any photos in our possession of the actual reunion in Buffalo but it was sure to be jubilant for Art. Reveling in the first hug and kiss with my mother. Seeing his mother for the first time since his dad died. Noting how big young brother Bob had grown, now in high school. Hearing nieces and nephews who could barely talk when Art left, now talking away with the innocence of a child.

To go from terror-filled skies over Germany to warm embraces of family in the old neighborhood must have been surreal. Settling into the old bedroom on 20 Columbus that first night home probably resulted in little sleep as all that Art had experienced ran through his mind. He must have let out the biggest sigh of relief yet that night, spared, safe and finally back to planning for the future.

But likely there were shadows across the ceiling as well while he tossed in bed, shadows blurred by tears as he remembered comrades lost and felt the absence of his father in the family home for the first time. As good as it must have been to be home, he likely felt the absence of Ernie and fellow crewmen, as well as Father Rice. I wonder if Padre Pio was with him that night? If not in spirit, in comforting memories of the wonders Art experienced in San Giovanni thousands of miles away.

OF COURSE, THE letters stopped when my father made it safely back to Buffalo. To continue the story from here, I draw on my own memory, the memories of family members and the stories we heard while Art was alive.

Once home, my father began to pick up where he left off over two and a half years earlier. He enrolled in college on the GI Bill, and earned an accounting degree from Canisius College in Buffalo in 1948. My parents were married that same year, and their first child, my brother David, was born in 1949.

My parents lived the classic post-World War II life in America. He went to work as an accountant for a large steel plant in Buffalo. She stayed home and raised the kids, including Marilyn, born in 1950, and Joanne, who debuted in 1953. That year, after living in apartments on Buffalo's East Side, Art and Ruth built a house in the suburbs. Not long after, a habit left over from the war caught up with my father.

RETURN OF PNEUMONIA

Art often spoke of how freely cigarettes were distributed to the soldiers in World War II. Smoke 'em if you got 'em. The airmen even smoked aboard the B-17, using the oxygen to keep the cigarettes lit. He became a heavy smoker. That, on top of the pneumonia he suffered during his stateside training, resulted in much damage to his lungs. In fact, he ended up in the hospital with pneumonia again in 1947, spending two weeks recovering at Buffalo's Sisters of Charity Hospital.

By 1957, with a new house and four kids, including an infant son, Paul, born in 1956, pneumonia struck again. Only this time it was far worse. An infection had set in and he underwent surgery at the Buffalo VA Hospital that resulted in more than half of the lung on his right side being removed. I remember summers at the beach as a kid tracing that surgery scar from just below his upper arm all the way down to his belt line. It was not a simple procedure.

Earlier in 1957, Art's brother Carl passed away from cancer. Carl left his wife and three children, all under the age of 10. The struggles of a world war were slowly fading in my father's memory, now replaced by the strains of losing his beloved older brother and the stress of persistent health problems.

But with the same resolve he had as a soldier – the same tailwinds – he drew on his faith – perhaps in prayers to Padre Pio – my mother's love and his family to carry on. Not only did he pull through from the lung surgery, he and my mom went on to have three more children. Lucky for my sister, Susan, born in 1960; me born in 1961; and my sister, Terese, the last to arrive in 1965.

Art continued to crunch numbers at the steel plant and provided a steady hand to guide the family at home.

CHAPTER 36 – FAMILY MAN

Art, Ruth and family. L to R: Susan, on Marilyn's lap, Martin, Terese, David, Paul and Joanne.

GROWING UP, I never really thought about being the child of a World War II veteran. As a boy, I remember thinking it was pretty cool that he flew in a plane during the war, but I never really grasped the importance of his experience until I was much older.

Like most veterans, my father did not speak a lot about the war. And like most returning soldiers, all he wanted to do was to get back to some sense of normalcy. His large family helped him do that.

No surprise, we all attended Catholic grammar school and high school. As kids, we knew about my father meeting Padre Pio, but I can't honestly say the saint was central to our upbringing. I do believe, however, each of us was influenced by the saint in one way or another, as he was certainly influential on my father's continuing faith.

When Padre Pio passed in 1968, my father would have definitely spoke about him, but I was just seven years old, and would not have understood. It was only in the 1990s, when Padre Pio was beatified and on the way to sainthood that my father really began to talk about his visits to San Giovanni Rotondo.

LOTS OF LOVE

WE WERE A large family, but each child was made to feel special. My father loved filming everything with his 8 mm movie camera. Watching those old home movies now, I am struck by how many birthday celebrations they had, in reel after reel. My mother always had a cake and my father would flick on these bright camera lights that could illuminate an airport runway, capturing it on movie film – with no sound – as everyone sang happy birthday. We were all left permanently squinting because of those lights.

My father took a week off every summer and the family of nine would pile into the old yellow Mercury station wagon to vacation in a rented cabin in New York's Allegheny State Park or to his old friend Gordon Schilling's summer cottage south of Buffalo. We didn't have a lot of money but it never felt like we lacked anything.

Whatever my parents did, they did it for love of family and each other. It seems to have been a good formula. All seven children graduated from college, paying our own tuition and learning that if we wanted something, we worked for it. We all married and had children, giving our parents a total of 18 grandchildren, and my mother one great grandchild when she was alive. Perfect upbringing? Of course not. But I wouldn't trade it for all the money in the world. I thank Art and Ruth every day.

KEEPING THE FAITH

THE STEEL PLANT closed in the early 1980s and my father was out of a job at 59 years old. He mustered on, taking a part-time accounting job with a county heating assistance program where he worked until he retired at age 62. When the steel company asked if he wanted monthly distributions for his pension or one lump sum, my father wisely took the lump sum. A few years later, the company went into bankruptcy and monthly pensions were drastically cut.

In retirement, my father became even more active in his church, counting Sunday collections, serving as a Eucharistic minister, filling in as an usher when needed, and simply helping out wherever he could. He still had the same helpful spirit that led him to assist Father Rice in his office during the war. I believe Padre Pio was also responsible for strengthening that spirit as the mystic's popularity grew in the 1990s.

My parents took a couple of trips to the National Centre for Padre Pio located south of Allentown, Pennsylvania. After Art passed, we found numerous books on Padre Pio in his basement library, and many bookmarked web sites related to the saint on Art's computer.

My father and my mother were also able to travel in retirement, visiting my brother in Arizona, my sister in Spain, where she taught on a U.S. naval base, and taking trips to 463rd Bomb Group reunions across the United States.

CHAPTER 37 – FOREVER FLYBOYS

Arizona reunion - 2002

I WAS SITTING with my father on an airliner headed to a 463rd Bomb Group reunion in Arizona. My brother, Paul, and my mother sat across the aisle from us. When the airline pilot kicked in the engines, my father turned to me and said, "I always hated that sound. It meant we were really going."

For the first time, I really understood the dread he must have felt before each mission. It was frighteningly obvious when the engines started that the mission had begun. On that trip, I really began to understand what a privilege it is to be the child of a World War II veteran.

My dad began to attend reunions of the 463rd Bomb Group veterans in the 1980s. They were held every year in different cities across the country. He reconnected with Ernie Conrad, Bill Dean and others, including Father Rice in 1988. My mother was able to finally meet Father Rice in person during that reunion.

I am forever grateful to have had the chance to join these veterans in Arizona in 2002, although by that time Bill stopped coming to the reunions, and Ernie and Father Rice had passed away.

Throughout the reunion, the veterans shared yellowing photographs and told funny stories of their airmen days. There were colorful yarns of how they kept their sanity in the idle hours between missions. There were sad accounts of downed planes and lost fellow airmen. I wrote about the experience in an article published in a Buffalo newspaper. Several veterans sent me letters thanking me for writing the article and showing in an interest in their stories. A number of them said they feared being forgotten as the years passed.

That was 18 years ago and most, if not all, of these veterans are gone. No longer here to tell those stories. Leaving it up to the generations that followed to preserve their memory and the lessons of the war they fought. I hope I have helped to do so in some way with this story.

Chapter 38 – Reunion with St. Pio

"You know I never told you about that German guy," my father said looking at me with a momentary spark of lucidity.

"Oh yeah, Dad? What's that?" I asked.

"I saw him coming, I lined him up, and I took him out."

He slipped back into sleep before I could ask what he meant. But he had said the exact same thing to my brother the night before.

Was this some sort of deathbed confession from the aged veteran? Could it have been on the Berlin mission when the crews noted shooting down at least one if not several of the German 262s that attacked? He never spoke about it before, but I imagine he would have felt terrible knowing he took another life, even if it was in combat. Such was his Catholic faith.

Never mind that the bombs dropped during his missions probably killed hundreds if not thousands of Germans. However, he didn't see those deaths from high in the air.

I'm not sure there is any way to confirm what my father said. But I hope it gave him some relief to get it off his chest if he really did shoot down a German fighter. It would have been just like him to keep it secret all those years, not boastful, but rather shameful. He killed someone. An emotional injury from the war always hidden from us.

The final flight

In his last years, my father suffered from dementia and was in physical decline. My parents still lived in the house they built in 1953 and with lots of teamwork among their children and grandchildren, the family was able to care for them at home. Art reached his 90th birthday in November of 2012. I got a call from my mother on the following New Year's Day. My father had fallen and was very confused.

When I arrived at their home, his legs were wedged under their bed and any attempt to move him was met with cries of pain. I called 911 and an ambulance took my father to the Veterans Administration hospital in Buffalo. That's where he told me about "that German guy".

The decline continued and hospice care at the VA would see him through to the end of his life. During his time there, my father would often look out at the ceiling of his hospital room and call out "Carl" or "Norm". Once he told me he was trying to get their attention but they would not answer. Was it just the delusion of dementia or were his brothers waiting there to welcome him home? I think they *were* there. And what occurred after Art's passing makes me think St. Pio welcomed him, too.

The relic

My father passed on a Friday in January of 2013. My siblings and I watched with incredible pride as his flagged draped body was escorted out of the VA hospice wing to the salutes of other teary-eyed veterans in the hallway. Such respect as he went off into the wild blue yonder one more time.

As my family planned for the funeral, St. Pio seemed to make his presence known.

One of Padre Pio's most recognizable quotes – *"Pray, hope, and don't worry*" – was included on the front cover of a funeral program we created, a tribute to my father's connection to the saint.

The Sunday after my father's passing, my brother, Paul, and sister, Terese, took our mother to mass at her church, Infant of Prague. A visiting priest was saying the mass and as he began his homily, he started talking about Saint Pio. My brother and sister smiled incredulously at one another, acknowledging the timely coincidence. Paul went and introduced himself to the priest after mass, telling him how our father had just passed and had many encounters with Padre Pio during World War II.

The priest looked stunned. "Wait here one minute," the priest said to my brother.

The priest hurried out of the church and returned from his car with a small, ornate bronze figurine. It was a relic of Padre Pio, a piece of one of the fingerless gloves the priest wore to cover the wounds in his hands. "I want you to have this at your father's wake and funeral," the priest said excitedly. "And just bring it back here when you are done."

My family and I saw this as so much more than a coincidence. We had Padre Pio's relic at the wake and it was a centerpiece of conversation, offering comfort and hope. At the funeral, the relic echoed that hope, during a mass celebrated by a family priest who spoke of my father being reunited with Padre Pio.

Pray, hope and don't worry. I gave the eulogy for my father, centered on that quote, eying the relic near the casket as I spoke. I'm not much of a public speaker, but the words seemed to come to me naturally, without any of the nervousness I would typically feel giving presentations and so forth for my job in advertising.

After my father's death, Padre Pio seemed to make himself known to my family more and more often. One day, shortly after Art's funeral, my mom asked me to get one of her hats out of the coat closet. As I grabbed a box on a top shelf, an old prayer card featuring Padre Pio floated down, landing on top of my foot with the mystic's image facing up. The logical person in me understands that the card was long on the shelf and just happened to fall off when I moved the box. The person who saw that card with Padre Pio looking up at me sees more meaning in the experience.

Another time, my daughter was helping to clean up in the basement of my mom's house when a note, handwritten by my father, seemed to just appear out of a stack of old papers with the words "pray, hope and don't worry".

Those are small examples and I can identify with the skeptics who would call them coincidences. Nonetheless, the comfort they brought was real. Other experiences seemed much more than coincidental, as well.

CHAPTER 39 – THE CLOUDS

Sunsets over Lake Erie on a summer night in Buffalo are often spectacular. A couple of years back – in the early stages of putting this book together – my wife and I were enjoying what she likes to call Water Wednesdays. Every Wednesday in the summer, we pick a place to have dinner on the water, taking advantage of the cool breezes, bright sunsets and a midweek break after work.

This particular Wednesday we ate outside on the patio of a restaurant down by Buffalo's outer harbor, with a clear view of the setting sun. As we dined, I was telling my wife about some correspondence I found from the early 1990s between my father and a Capuchin priest, Reverend John Schug, of Springfield, Massachusetts.

Father Schug had written a book on Padre Pio and was working on a second one, when apparently he had reached out to my father to ask about his experiences with the saint during the war. I do not know how they made their initial connection.

My father sent the priest copies of photos that he had from the monastery in San Giovanni Rotondo – the same photos found in this book – and in a return thank you letter, Father Schug referenced some well-known stories involving Padre Pio and Allied pilots during the war.

As the stories went, the Allied pilots – both American and British – reported being being waved off by a monk in the clouds who was flying right in front of their planes with his arms extended out and his hands open and facing them. The pilots did not complete their missions because the flying monk kept preventing them from bombing the area. There were often mysterious malfunctions, causing the bombs to drop harmlessly in the fields, or mechanical failures that caused the planes to veer off course. Father Schug was trying to confirm these stories but so far had found no one who could give him a first person account.

Interestingly, my father wrote the priest again and explained why he believed the stories might just be village of San Giovanni folklore.

"In regard to the story of Padre Pio's intercession on behalf of the town, I would like to offer you my thoughts on it. Do not interpret it as a denial of Padre Pio. Having experienced his presence, there is no way I could doubt him or anything about him. San Giovanni may or may not have been occupied by the Germans. I do not know. It certainly was on very high ground and may have been used for observing the plain below but it was not important as a highly defended objective.

"Having observed from the heights the bombardment and destruction imposed on Foggia below them on the plain, perhaps the occupants of San Giovanni could only marvel at being spared a similar fate. An attack on Foggia by Allied fighter aircraft would have come from the east over the San Giorgio mountains where San Giovanni lay. The fighters would have appeared over the town at a very low and scary altitude. The situation, to say the least, was very frightful for the occupants and they were grateful to God and his servant Padre Pio for escaping the suffering down below. I am not saying the story is a lie, but just the reaction of a grateful people." – Art

At dinner, I was explaining to my wife how I found it interesting that my father was somewhat skeptical – or at least logical – in his correspondence with the American priest. My guess is Art wanted to set the record straight that the Allies did not – and would not – bomb Padre Pio's village. After all, the airman had been there and on the long journey up the mountain.

After dinner, in the car on the way home, Sue began reviewing the many sunset photos she had taken on her phone. As she flipped through them she suddenly said, "Wow. This is amazing. There is a clear face of a man forming in the clouds."

She showed me one of the more detailed photos and I could not believe what I was seeing. That clear face in the clouds was Padre Pio. Others may have seen Albert Einstein, but to me, it was another sign of St. Pio's presence.

Reproduction of the photo in print may result in less definition to the face in the clouds, but it can still be made out at top center.

When we got home we compared her photo to the photo on the cover of a book on Padre Pio I had recently read. The likeness was uncanny. I can be as skeptical as the next person, but it almost seemed as if Padre Pio was telling us to believe those pilot stories. Or perhaps it was my father admitting he was wrong and Padre Pio did appear to Allied pilots in the clouds. Regardless, it happened to my wife and me. And again, the sense of comfort – and wonder – was real.

CHAPTER 40 – INFLUENCE OF THE SAINT

THERE HAS ALWAYS been something pushing me to write my father's story. I loved the man, so that is certainly part of it. He was also a great influence when it came to giving back and helping people in need – a tenet of Padre Pio.

In the 1970s, I remember going with my father to assist in delivering food with the local St. Vincent DePaul Society to Vietnamese refugees who had come to Buffalo to escape the Vietnam War. We delivered bags of groceries and despite a complete language barrier, my father's goodness connected with the families. His smile and gentle manner seemed to put them at ease and give them hope. I remember how that really struck me.

Inspired by my father, I have always tried to do the right thing, to help others and to act according to the Christian values I was taught. I have failed many times and in many ways. But something always makes me keep trying and leads me to experiences that change the direction of my life. I've come to believe it is Padre Pio, channeled through my father, one of the saint's American spiritual children. Here's a good example.

THE MISSION.

A few years back, my work as a freelance writer took me to St. Luke's Mission of Mercy in Buffalo, a Catholic mission that provides food, clothing and shelter for the poor and underserved on the city's East Side. Founded by Norm Paolini and Amy Betros in 1993, the mission, as the name implies, is centered on mercy, alleviating the suffering of others. Locally, Amy is thought by many to be a mystic herself, graced with the ability to share great love, help heal people and bring them closer to God.

I came to the mission to interview Mike Taheri for a Canisius College magazine article I was writing – an alumni profile, as Mike is a graduate of the school – and we met at the dining hall at St. Luke's. A prominent attorney in Buffalo, Mike had cut back on a successful law practice and retired from teaching at the University at Buffalo Law School to volunteer his time in helping the mission serve the poor. As the interview progressed, I couldn't help but notice an illustration of Padre Pio hanging on the wall in the dining hall. There were other pieces of religious artwork on the walls, but my eyes kept returning to St. Pio, as though the saint was staring right at me.

Mike's genuine and sincere manner and the presence of the Padre Pio illustration gave me a distinct feeling that St. Luke's was a special place. Little did I know at the time how special the mission would become for me.

A few weeks after that interview, Mike called and asked if I would help him with an adult men's reading group at St. Luke's. He formed the group with Sam Tillman, a former member of a street gang in Buffalo, to help men who never finished high school improve their reading skills and pursue high school equivalency certificates. Mike thought I might be able to help with the men with writing skills. I barely knew Mike and I'd never been involved in anything like the group, but despite some reluctance, felt a strong draw to join in.

While the group met at night, Mike then asked me to volunteer to teach an English language arts class for sixth, seventh and eighth graders at St. Luke's Catholic school. Essentially a home school known as our Lady of Hope, Mike is instrumental in seeing that students in the school graduate from eighth grade and go on to a Catholic high school. He finds sponsors to cover high school tuition and stays in touch with each student, encouraging them to go on to college.

I resisted Mike's request to teach, reminding him that I was a writer, not a teacher. He said it would it would only be for three months, until the end of the school year. I continued to make excuses, but felt a tug to give it a try. Maybe it was Mike. He can be very persuasive. I gave in. Besides, I thought, what's three months?

I ended up teaching the class for nearly three years. And I realized, we are all teachers, meant to share the skills that God gives us. St. Luke's changed me. I think I learned more from that experience than the students in class. About compassion, gratitude, community, and so much more. I helped chaperone class trips to Washington, D.C., Boston, Massachusetts and Williamsburg, Virginia, all places I had never been. I worked with wonderful, faithful people I now call friends.

I've come to sincerely believe that Padre Pio led me to St. Luke's to teach. Then St. Luke's led me to another Padre Pio experience.

CHAPTER 41 – LOCAL MIRACLE

IN 2018, I WAS still teaching at St. Luke's. One day I arrived for class and was walking down a school hallway when I noticed an article posted on a bulletin board. The local Catholic paper reported that a traveling exhibit of Padre Pio – Saint Pio – relics was coming to the Buffalo area. As I read the article, I recognized the names of the couple who would be co-chairing the exhibit, Mike and Maureen. I did not know them very well but we belonged to the same parish and had spoken a few times.

I sent an e-mail to Mike to tell him my father had met Padre Pio during the war and that I had some photos of the saint if he was interested. Not only were Mike and Maureen interested, they invited my wife and me to a private showing of the relics in their home. It was thrilling.

There were gloves and other items, however, the relic that caused me most pause was a cloak of Padre Pio. There's a good chance it is the same cloak shown in the photos in this book. My father may have seen the same cloak during his visits with Padre Pio during the war. I felt a great sense of peace and comfort in seeing it myself.

At the showing, Mike and Maureen shared their own experience with Padre Pio. About 20 years ago, Maureen was pregnant with their son, one of their six children. A sonogram at the time resulted in some distressing news – the doctor told the couple there were cysts on the baby's brain, and if he survived, he would likely be disabled.

Going home with the sad news, Mike decided he was going to devote himself to prayer to Padre Pio. Mike wasn't sure why he chose the priest – Padre Pio had not yet been canonized a saint. But Mike had heard of miracles attributed to the Capuchin priest and prayed with all his might, constantly, asking for help for his soon-to-be born son.

A few weeks went by when, one evening, Mike and Maureen had retired to bed. Exhausted from the pregnancy, Maureen fell right to sleep. As Mike lay in bed praying, he was suddenly hit with a strong smell of flowers, as though a perfume bottle had been sprayed throughout the room, as he described it. He woke Maureen up who quickly noted the sweet aroma as well. Checking the room to see if something had spilled or if a window was open letting in some sweet scented air, they found nothing.

A couple of weeks later, Mike and Maureen went for their next sonogram, as the baby's due date was approaching. When they met with the doctor after the sonogram, he had a puzzled look on his face. He told them there was no longer any sign of the cysts. And he could not explain why. Mike and Maureen looked at one another and smiled because they knew why.

Their son was born healthy and happy. He was there, smiling brightly, during the showing of the Padre Pio relics. Having graduated from college, he is currently attending medical school to become a doctor. Mike and Maureen said they gratefully owe it all to Padre Pio – St. Pio.

"YOU KNOW, I have a ritual, too. Every night before I go to sleep, I say that prayer you sent me from Lincoln once – a civilian's prayer for a soldier. Then I hop into bed, take one last look at the picture of you and I on the dresser, turn out the light and off I am to dreamland.

"So you see, my last waking thoughts and prayers are of you and for you. It's almost time to perform that ritual now, so I will say good-night sweetheart. I love you. Always." – Ruth

In an earlier chapter, in one of his letters to my mother, my dad wrote about Mary Pyle and how she told him and his fellow choir members that Padre Pio is known for bringing couples together. Art encouraged Ruth to pray to Padre Pio that they might be a married couple some day. It obviously worked, and they were married for nearly 64 years.

I also noted earlier how my parents' letters were sometimes corny, but that may just be colored by my perception some 70+ years later. In fact, re-reading the letters provided a good study in how love can progress and grow. Distance certainly made their hearts grow fonder, and as trials and tribulations of war and life rained on and on, my parents' love rooted deeper.

Early letters, when my father was still stateside training, were more casual, with my father signing off with a simple "As ever, Art". This was a popular closing that seemed to express modest affection. By 1944 and 1945, the letters gushed with romantic closings and sign-offs, an indication of how much they missed one another and how much stronger their love had grown in the rigors of the war.

Truth is, their expressions of love are quite beautiful and reminders of what we have lost along with the art of writing letters. If my father's meeting of Padre Pio inspired those expressions, all the better.

With all due respect to their privacy, I didn't want to close this book without noting a few examples from their letters. After all, it was the letters that made the book possible. I think they would understand.

"There's a beautiful moon out tonight. Wish we could enjoy it together. Tell you what I'll do. It's ten o'clock here now, so it's five back there. I'll give him a message for you now and in a few hours, when he is over Buffalo, when you look up at him, you'll see that message. Know what that message is? I love you. I love you. I love you. And if someone else should happen to see it, I'll not be sorry, for if you know it applies only to you, I don't care if the whole world knows it!" – Art

"The weather has turned quite warm and there is a big moon which lights up the sky. Kind of reminds me of those nights in June. Oh, sweet memories those are. A full moon always starts me reminiscing. I always think of you and wonder where you are and what you're doing at that moment when I'm talking to Mr. Moon. He's a big comfort to me, that man in the moon. I know he watches over my love seven thousand miles away and the next night he's over here watching over me." – Ruth

"Before I close this letter, I want to quote you something from the Catholic Digest Magazine which is most appropriate and may be of some consolation to you as it was to me. 'Life has taught us that love does not consist in gazing at each other, but in looking outward together in the same direction.' I love you darling, very much." – Art

"No need to tell you what the prayer in my heart is, Art. Dear Lord, please take care of my love, and next year, please let him be here beside me. Forever and always." – Ruth

"Remember my sweetest darling that I love you with all my heart and soul. Goodnight sweetheart. I'll dream of you." – Art

"You know that's what I am always looking forward to, that day when we will be together for ever and ever. And you know, too, that I love you so very much and miss you more each day. Good night dearest. God bless you and keep you safe." – Ruth

"Let me quote you something from a story I read today: 'In the cottage that had been the woodsman's they had a wonderful honeymoon. No king and queen in any palace of gold were happier than they. For them, their tiny cottage was a palace, and the flowers that filled their garden were their couriers. Long and careless and full of kisses were the days of their reign.' Like it? I did. I love you with all the devotion I can muster." – Art

Chapter 43 – Lessons learned

In working on this book, I learned a lot – about the war, about my dad, my mother, and even about myself. Reading the letters, I tried to put myself in my father's place. Nothing I have ever done in my life comes close to his experience so it was hard to imagine.

But the more I read, the better my understanding of what it was like. And the better my understanding of what made my parents tick. Here are some of the lessons I learned from them – the tailwinds perhaps we can all use on our passage through life.

Love never dies

It's in every letter. My parents kept their love alive through the written word, through some trying times. Love continued through a marriage of 64 years, with ups and downs along the way. And that love has never died... even after they passed.

They are still loved by me, my family and friends here on earth, perhaps even more than ever. After all, absence does make the heart grow fonder. And I am sure Art and Ruth love us wherever they are. There are times I can just feel it.

The love expressed in their letters – still living on the pages – reminds me of the love from which I was born and that they gave us as a family. That love inspired me and guided me in writing this story. It is alive. It is up to us to tend to that love and make it flourish.

Family matters

My father lost his dad and continued to fight in a war. My grandmother lost her husband and worried about two other sons in that same war. My mother worried every day Art was gone. What pulled them through was strength of family.

The importance of family was passed on from my grandparents to my parents and to me and my siblings. Of course, I never knew my grandfather Haumesser but I carry on with what he helped start by coming to America. I hope my own children feel that family strength. It is a gift never to be taken for granted and it matters.

Faith works

It certainly worked for my father, fueled by his meeting of Padre Pio, and taken on every mission.

Of course, Art raised his children in a strict Catholic household. I didn't always understand it, having been taught a lot of rite and ritual without a lot of explanation in grammar school and high school.

But I began to understand a little better as I wrote this book. While my father followed all the rules of Catholic hierarchy at the time, his true faith was within – that is what he leaned on.

For various reasons, I no longer agree with the rules, but writing this, I rediscovered my own faith within. Sure, the basis of that faith was formed in a dozen years of Catholic school. But my father's connection to Padre Pio and some of the incidents I have described serve to bring my belief in God into sharper focus.

There is something waiting for us after this life. Have faith, however you perceive God. Pray, hope and don't worry. It works.

Keep pushing

Pneumonia. Fifty-three days in a military hospital. Failure at pilot school. His father's death. Terrors of war. My father faced some obstacles during his military service, to say the least. But through it all, he kept pushing. After the war, he had pneumonia again and ultimately major surgery for a lung infection.

His cherished older brother, Carl, died that same year from cancer. Art would lose his other two brothers to cancer in the years that followed. He pushed through. Late in life, diagnosed with diabetes, followed by dementia, somehow he stayed positive. Whenever I wallow in some minor inconvenience, I think of him. And I find the spirit to keep moving forward.

HAVE PATIENCE

MY MOTHER ALWAYS said patience is a virtue. Amen. She certainly learned a lot about patience during the war. Waiting for letters from Art. Waiting for him to return safely, delay after delay. My father, too, had to have patience, as did every soldier, not knowing what was ahead and when the war would be over.

I thought about this a lot during the coronavirus pandemic of 2020. It helped to remember what previous generations endured and how they must have developed the patience necessary to cope. I am working on being more patient every day.

ACCEPT IT

LIFE CAN BE tough. Accept it. But it can also be so beautiful. Accept it. When my father washed out of pilot school and navigator training, he accepted that it wasn't meant to be. But he made the best of his situation and encountered life-changing experiences. That's what I learned about acceptance. Not that you let life walk all over you. Rather, you take what you have been given, with gratitude, accept it, share it and make the most of it. You never know where acceptance may lead.

ACKNOWLEDGE MYSTERIES

NOT EVERYTHING CAN be explained. Padre Pio's stigmata, for example. Doctors, popes, theologians, and many wise scholars refer to the Italian priest's wounds as a mystery. There is so much in this world we can not begin to understand.

Was the relic at my father's funeral just a coincidence? Did Padre Pio perform a miracle for Mike and Maureen and their newborn son? Was that Padre Pio in the clouds over Buffalo? Mysterious, for sure, but that does not mean we can't believe. In saints. In miracles. In God. We can believe and hope to have a better understanding some day.

CHAPTER 44 – WHAT EVER HAPPENED TO...

THEY HAVE ALL passed away, but here's a brief follow-up on what happened to my mother, grandmother and others who played a role in this story.

Ruth Haumesser

"Know what I'm doing tonight? Looking through all the letters I ever received from you. No, I didn't read them all. Heavens, it would take weeks! Gosh, what a stack of letters. Someday, I'm going to read all of them over again." – Ruth

Ruth worked for the Iroquois Gas Company while waiting for my father's return from the war. She married my father in 1948 after he had earned an accounting degree from Canisius College. She raised seven children while my father worked as an accountant at a steel plant in South Buffalo. When the youngest three kids were in high school – myself included – Ruth went back to work as an administrative assistant for Erie County.

She sang in her church choir and stayed close with a group of four or five women she knew since high school – Club, she called it. Ruth had eighteen grandchildren and a great grandchild and enough love for every one of them. She was the sweetest mom a person could ever have. I'm not sure if she ever did sit down and read all those letters over again. I'm glad I did. She passed away at 93. Love you, mom.

Anna Haumesser

MY GRANDMOTHER IS just 53 years old in this photo, evidence of how losing her husband and having three sons fighting in the war sped the aging, weary signs of a trying life. But she was a special woman who carried on with quiet strength until her boys were all home. Born Anna Mary Hartman in Buffalo, NY, she worked in the family bakery into adulthood and married my grandfather in 1912.

They had seven children – including Leora, a daughter who passed at the age of two in 1929 – 27 grandchildren, and ultimately, more than 50 great grandchildren, most of whom she never knew here on earth. She went to live with my Aunt Virginia and Uncle Ray Petty after the war.

I have many fond memories of visiting their home and being greeted warmly by my grandmother who would spend winters in Florida with her cousin Barb, and always bring back oranges for us.

When Anna passed in 1971 at the age of 79, it was the first time I experienced the sadness of a death in the family. I could only imagine the magnified sadness of loss she must have felt for her young daughter, eldest son and husband. My wife and I proudly named our daughter after her.

Carl Haumesser, right

CARL HAUMESSER LED an army intelligence unit in the European theater in World War II. He was engaged to Anne Madden during the war and they married in September of 1945 when he returned.

Carl would come home and serve as a Lieutenant Colonel in the New York National Guard where he was commander of the Second Battalion of the 174th Regiment, 27th Armored Division. He and Anne had a daughter and two sons and settled in a suburb of Buffalo.

Having graduated from Canisius College in Buffalo prior to the war, Carl attended law school at the University of Buffalo while working for the U.S. Post Office. He died of cancer in 1957 before finishing his law degree. He was 42 years old. My father would try to repay the debt he felt to his older brother by looking out for Carl's children and widow. My Aunt Anne would also pass from cancer in 1972.

Father George Rice

FATHER RICE WAS transferred from the 463rd to another unit as the war wound down. When the war was over and he returned to the U.S., he tried to visit the families of every U.S. soldier in the 463rd who were missing in action or had died in the war.

He stayed in touch with my father when he returned to the U.S. and lived in Southern California. My parents visited with him during a couple of the 463rd Bomb Group's reunions in the 1980s and 1990s.

The photo here was taken by my sister, Joanne, who took a cross country trip in her sky blue Volkswagen Beetle in 1977 and visited Father Rice in Palm Springs, California. She described him as very kind and pastoral, saying he had high praise for our dad. Father Rice passed away in 1996 in Palm Springs. He was 86 years old.

Padre Pio – St. Pio of Pietrelcina

PADRE PIO PASSED away in 1968 at the age of 81. He is buried in San Giovanni Rotondo in a crypt in the Church of Our Lady of Grace. His funeral was attended by more than 100,000 people. It was reported by those who were with him when he died that the stigmata had completely disappeared at his passing.

Pope John Paul II canonized Padre Pio of Pietrelcina in 2002. More than 300,000 people braved stifling heat as they filled St. Peter's Square and nearby streets to witness the canonization. It is considered one of the largest religious ceremonies in history.

There are a number of informative books on Padre Pio which I list in the references. Since his canonization, his popularity continues to grow around the world. He has faithful admirers and followers, even including Protestants, Buddhists, and Hindus. There are more than 200 monuments and shrines around the world dedicated to St. Pio, including in Buffalo, where a Catholic church on Hertel Avenue installed a large statue of him surrounded by benches where people can sit and pray, hope…and not worry.

Ernie Conrad

ERNIE CONRAD AND my father exchanged Christmas cards every year and they eventually caught up with one another at the yearly 463rd reunions. Ernie had been married before he was drafted and my father once said his friend went AWOL to visit his wife when they were stationed at Fort Dix, New Jersey.

He did not get caught and Ernie went on to raise a family in Brooklyn. The former crew members lost touch as age caught up. Ernie passed away in 2000. Unfortunately, my father received word of his death too late to attend the funeral. I sure would have like to have met Ernie.

The Army Air Corps

Off we go into the wild blue yonder,
Climbing high into the sun;
Here they come zooming to meet our thunder;
At 'em boys, giv 'er the gun!
Down we dive spouting our flame from under
Off with one helluva a roar!
We live in fame or go down in flame,
Nothing'll stop the Army Air Corps

WWII References

Caidin, Martin, *Flying Forts, The B-17 in World War II*, Ballantine Books, 1968

Jablonski, Edward, *Flying Fortresses*, Doubleday & Company, 1965

Rubin, Harold, *The Fighting 463rd – A Narrative and Pictorial History of the 463rd Bombardment Group*, 1946

463rd Bomb Group Historical Society Home Page – www.463RD.org

References for more on Padre Pio –
St. Pio of Pietrelcina

Rega, Frank M., *Padre Pio and America*, TAN Books, 2005

Allen, Diane, *Pray, Hope and Don't Worry, True Stories of Padre Pio, Book I*, Padre Pio Press, 2012

Ruffin, C. Bernard, *Padre Pio, The True Story*, Our Sunday Visitor Publishing Division, 1991

Schug, John A., OFM Cap, *A Padre Pio Profile*, St. Bede's Publications, 1987

www.saintpiofoundation.org

www.padrepio.com

About the Author

Martin Haumesser is the sixth child – and third son – of Art and Ruth Haumesser. Martin earned a bachelor's degree in journalism from State University College of New York at Buffalo and has worked as a writer in the advertising and public relations field for 37 years, the last 14 for his own business. Married with two adult children, he resides in a suburb of Buffalo, NY.

www.ingramcontent.com/pod-product-compliance
Lightning Source LLC
LaVergne TN
LVHW021509080426
835509LV00018B/2450